Building the Italian Renaissance

REACTING CONSORTIUM PRESS

This book is a "reacting" game. Reacting games
are interactive role-playing games in which students
are responsible for their own learning. Reacting games
are currently used at more than 400 colleges and
universities in the United States and abroad. Reacting
Consortium Press is a publishing program of the
Reacting Consortium, the association of schools
that use reacting games. For more information
visit http://reactingconsortiumpress.org.

Building the Italian Renaissance

BRUNELLESCHI'S DOME AND THE FLORENCE CATHEDRAL

PAULA KAY LAZRUS

REACTING
CONSORTIUM PRESS

ISBN 978-1-4696-5339-6 (pbk.: alk. paper)

ISBN 978-1-4696-5340-2 (ebook)

Cover illustration: Painting of the Piazza della Signoria in Florence by Bernardo Bellotto (1721–1780), Museum of Fine Arts, Budapest (Photo by Web Gallery of Art).

Distributed by the

University of North Carolina Press

116 South Boundary Street

Chapel Hill, NC 27514-3808

www.uncpress.org

Contents

Figures
and Tables

Building the Italian Renaissance

1

Introduction

This game focuses on the competition to complete the final phase of construction on the Cathedral of Santa Maria del Fiore in Florence in 1418. It was the great challenge of a generation of workers to figure out how to execute the dome designed by Nero di Fioravanti, a project that consumed the lives of many of Florence's citizens and that has provided food for thought and debate for many generations of Florentines, foreign scholars, and visitors. Throughout the nearly century and a quarter during which the cathedral was being built, Florence saw a period of enormous economic growth and prosperity, and with that came a desire to thank God for those riches through the construction of churches, chapels, hospitals, public civic buildings, and plazas filled with art. Sometimes these projects were little more than ways for the wealthy to display their power and intellectual bona fides. In other cases, works of art or buildings might demonstrate to the citizenship that a leader was grateful for his good fortune and/or to promote the ideals of the day. The distinctions we make today among disciplines as diverse as engineering and mathematics, philosophy and art were less acute during the period in question, one in which the basic concepts of what should be taught and what makes for a good citizen were in flux. The early Florentine projects represent the foundations leading to a flowering of art and culture that is known as the Renaissance, a period of intellectual and creative exploration that was grounded in an appreciation for human achievements, past and present, today referred to as humanism.[1] The game will allow you to investigate the intersection of the creative ideas, practical skills, and ideas about applying past knowledge to current problem sets

1. The term "humanism" is used in retrospect. It was not used at the time. It refers to the ideas derived from the study of classical culture and writing that led to the development of the idea that humans could lead rational, beneficial, and ethical lives that were not solely derived from the divine.

and their intersection with the newly articulated ideas about the development of a good society.

The early 1400s were a moment of scholarly ferment with new ideas emerging that were developed by intellectuals looking to understand how best to develop good citizens, citizens who are crucial to the healthy functioning of a republic that requires civic participation. Florence prided itself on the fact that it was an independent republic finding its roots in its original self-governing structure as a simple municipality in the twelfth century. It was proud of the fact that as it grew and prospered it did not fall to a prince or duke (at least until the sixteenth century), but rather remained independent, governed by its citizens even as it undertook to expand its territory to include other municipalities within the surrounding territory (such as Arezzo and Pisa).

This was also a time when many manuscripts from the Roman era once thought lost to common usage were beginning to come to light through chance discoveries in monastery libraries. They were being translated from Latin, Arabic, or Greek into Italian. Some of these challenged received wisdom from the past. Others provided information about methods and ideas that had vanished with time. In fact, several crucial ancient works had only just been rediscovered and made available for study at the time our game begins. A copy of Vitruvius's *De Architectura* (*On Architecture*) was uncovered in 1414 in Saint Gallen, Switzerland. It contained instructions for building the kinds of monuments that people could see (some in ruins) and marvel at. How, Florentines and others of the early Renaissance wondered, could the ancients have built these amazing structures? What tools did they use? It seemed almost impossible to some that people living so long ago could have constructed the immense temples and other buildings still visible in towns and in the countryside, and yet, there they stood for all to see. Today, we look back on the monuments of the past and think much the same thing. On the other hand, the new thinking of the period encouraged people to value

and exalt the skills and creativity of past individuals and try to apply it to current projects. Vitruvius not only wrote of the great ancient monuments and their proportions, decorations, and settings but provided information on the technologies used to build them. It is a key text for this game, as are the challenges facing those who wanted to see the dome completed. Those who would attempt to understand what Vitruvius was aiming for and apply it in their own work would be acting within the world of humanistic ideals.

The game is set in the period that the ideas that would become known as humanism were first being explored. Some people date the beginning of these ideas to the works of Petrarch in the 1330s. He wrote to convince people of the value of classical thinking as opposed to the then common reliance on the direction and faith of the church. This was quite contrary to the common way of thinking that did not look to the individual's contributions and worth as something developed by the individual but rather given by God. Some of the texts written roughly within the time frame of the game (early 1400s) developed ideas concerning what made Florence unique, or what made for a good citizen or a good society. They questioned earlier interpretations and ideas about how Florence was founded and what made for a strong civic society and proposed new ones. This questioning of received knowledge becomes fundamental to humanist thinking. Works like those written by Leonardo Bruni and Petrus Paulus Vergerius, which are among the texts for this game, provide some of the fundamental ideas and mindsets of Florentines at this critical moment.

Florence also had citizens whom today we might consider more practical in nature, that is, the artisans and the merchants; yet they too wrote important works. They wrote about art and about perspective (how to give the illusion of space in a painting or building), and they wrote about business and trade and foreign relations. In fact, the things that concern them in some cases still concern us today. One significant difference is that

Florentines in the early 1400s valued people with very broad skill sets. A businessman might also be a musician, or an artist, or if he were not so inclined, he might use his money to support the work of such people. Those who funded projects and commissioned art and architecture and music were patrons (supporters) of those fields. The artists themselves sought out these people in order to make a living. In sum, this idea that humans can contribute to the well-being of society from its social and economic foundations to its cultural expressions without divine intervention was fundamental to the new way of thinking.

Another major force in our game and within Florentine society at this time was its guilds. Artisans in a wide variety of fields were organized into groups by the labor they engaged in. They had to pass a review of their skills to be admitted, and once a part of the guild they were also, to a degree, responsible for one another, and to their city. The members of the guilds were also more than just painters, or wool workers, or carpenters. They had to have basic business knowledge to stay afloat and know how much to produce and whom to sell to. Some might also have been "chemists" (although the term didn't exist yet) because they needed to turn minerals into pigments for paints and dyes. Others might have been "architects" (although the term didn't exist yet), using their mathematical and engineering skills to design and build a wide variety of structures. Members of all guilds needed to be conversant enough in what we would consider business and political skills to govern their organizations and if their turn came, to serve in public office. Guilds were also commissioned to work on civic projects such as building churches and hospitals, and by 1418 they were often doing this work on behalf of the Florentine government. As a result they can be seen as important players within the city, and their members were respected members of the community. Today we live in a world where people are sometimes hyperspecialized. There is a reason we use the term "Renaissance man" or "Renaissance woman" for someone with wide-ranging curiosity and talent. It reflects the multiple levels of knowledge that people back then regularly acquired, most often by self-study and hands-on, just-see-if-it-works experience.

In this game you will become one of the members of this Florentine society. You may have to do research into several different fields in order to understand the ideas and the talents that your character requires, or to be able to ask probing questions of the teams who will be proposing plans for the final construction phase of the Cathedral of Santa Maria del Fiore—the dome. The heart of this game revolves around the Wool Guild's (Arte della Lana) search for a group that can propose how the dome might be constructed. The Wool Guild is one of the oldest and wealthiest of Florence's guilds and has been guiding this project for more than 100 years. The guild announced a competition to complete this major project, and a committee of Florentine citizens is gathered to help advise the guild in making a choice. All of you will be engaged either in presenting proposals for completing the dome or in judging that the proposals meet both the physical requirements (as laid out in the announcement asking for proposals) and the intellectual and aesthetic ideals of your beloved city. This may include exploring the importance of relatively new artistic techniques for creating perspective in paintings and how well ancient techniques are reflected in the construction or in exploring how larger ideas of knowledge or governing make Florence unique. The competition is not in fact about what the dome will look like, because that is already known from an existing model created by Neri di Fioravanti that sits in an aisle of the uncompleted church. The question is *how* it will be executed.

In this activity you are either members of one of three teams vying for the commission to build the dome or among the citizens who are deciding what will work best both for the building and for Florence and its reputation. The challenge for those who are members of the competing teams is to suggest how the work can be accomplished. For the other citizens it is to be informed enough to make a good decision bringing to bear the knowledge from each person's background as well as the greater ideas of the day. You will have to do research on what materials to use, how they might be standardized, how they might be hoisted into place, whether it is possible to work from multiple sides all at once, and so on. This may seem daunting, but as Tim Ingold has learned doing field work, "to know things you have to grow into them, and let them grow in you, so that they become a part of who you are."[2] His point is that what you learn through experience and action is deeper than what you learn by being told, and that experiential and active learning is at the heart of this activity. To figure out how this dome can be built and to advocate for your various positions, you will do research in order for you to feel confident either making a proposal or judging one. You can make models and test them out to see what stands or collapses. There are resources provided for you in the core texts for this game book, but you should feel inspired to go beyond and find more information. In this activity, as in much of life, Knowledge Is Power.

There is also the question of decoration and how the finished church and dome will fit in with the growing city's ideas and architecture. What will the decorative program for the dome be, if there even is one? How will it fit in with the rest of the church as construction on it finishes or with the baptistry across the plaza? Is the project too big or too flamboyant, perhaps casting a negative light on Florence? Does it favor the ingenuity of human genius over the divine, and is that a problem? The technical, artistic, and philosophical issues are what drive the game and should influence your decisions in making your proposal or selecting the winning one for constructing the dome. For a better idea of where key buildings and public spaces are located in Florence, please see figure 1.[3]

PROLOGUE: HOW TO BUILD THE DOME
The sun is shining and the air is warm and humid as you make your way down the narrow *Via dei Banchi* toward the Baptistry of San Giovanni. You are grateful for the shade given by overhanging balconies. How beautiful Florence is! Even though you have lived here all your life, you are continually amazed at the beautiful churches and public buildings, how the city's layout leads from cool streets to open sunny piazzas or even cooler churches where one can rest and admire the beautiful artwork that adorns them. The beauty you appreciate is the work of many local artisans and the foresight and hard work of your fellow citizens. It makes you feel good that Florence's position as a republic means you are personally invested in your city.

As you come upon the baptistry, you note its octagonal shape and the beautiful black and white marbles used in its construction. You stop a moment to see if any more work has been done on the big bronze doors. The goldsmith Lorenzo Ghiberti has been working to finish his commission for their decoration. There is still a lot to be done, you think. You turn, and look at the imposing façade of the Cathedral of Santa Maria del Fiore. How grand it is, and how spectacular its imposing bell tower designed by the painter Giotto di Bondoni (known simply as Giotto). It can be seen from almost anywhere in town. Even from the other side of the river! You have stood below it many a time, marveling at how it complements the simpler color scheme of the baptistry, and you always admire its beautiful use of green, red, and white stone. You love the panels on the lower levels of the tower, carved by Andrea Pisano, that represent different aspects of what makes a man, from his activities (professions), virtues, and

2. Tim Ingold, *Making: Anthropology, Archaeology, Art and Architecture* (London: Routledge, 2013), 1.

3. All images, maps, and drawings are taken, elaborated on, or drawn by the author unless otherwise noted.

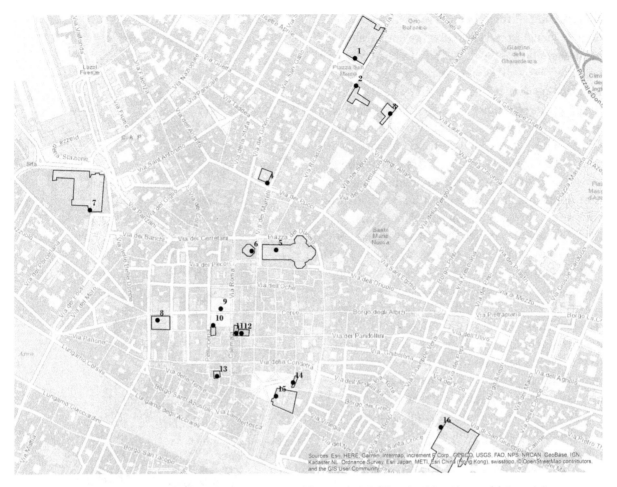

FIGURE 1 Florence: key locations. (1) Church of San Marco. (2) Ex Ospedale Church of San Mateo. (3) Ospedale degli Innocenti. (4) Palazzo Medici. (5) Santa Reparata/Santa Maria del Fiore. (6) Baptistry. (7) Ospedale San Paolo. (8) Palazzo Strozzi. (9) Ex Mercato Vecchio San Minato. (10) Approximate spot of the Arte de Medici e Speziale. (11) Palazzo dell'Arte della Lana. (12) Orsanmichele. (13) Palazzo dell'Arte della Seta. (14) Tribunale della Mercanzia. (15) Signoria/Palazzo Vecchio. (16) Santa Croce. For a more interactive version that allows for zooming in, go to the website ArcGis.com and search for "Florence SJU." Then select the item called Florence Key Sites 1400s and Web Mapping Application.

religious grounding to his education (in the liberal arts).

You have heard your family say that over the years many prominent artists and architects have worked on this project, something that you and your fellow citizens are very happy to point out to those who visit your city. What other place would have such distinguished artists working on such a civic project? You are proud to be a Florentine citizen and to be involved in discussions about the upcoming commission to construct the dome. It's a daunting task, you think, even for you, a fairly well-educated silk seller, and yet there are some technical details that seem hard to grasp. That said, Florence is very fortunate to have the works of such famous people right there for all to enjoy. You step inside the cool, dark doorway of the church to see how work is proceeding.

After more than 100 years, Florence's monumental Cathedral of Santa Maria del Fiore is still under construction. Things are moving along well, you note. In fact, it would seem that the one thing that needs work now is the dome. What a huge gaping hole there is over the spot where the nave and the transept meet. The pilasters at the sides of each of the octagonal sections rise 140 feet into the air, plus another thirty for the blocks on which the dome will spring. That seems so far away. The workers who will build this must not be afraid of heights, you think. Working up there would make you more than a little nervous. More questions start flooding your mind: How will they hoist the materials up there and maneuver them into place? Where will they keep extra materials for such a large project? What happens if the rate of building and the supply of materials are not in sync? This seems to be a major logistical undertaking. You don't envy your friends in the Arte della Lana (Wool Guild) who are overseeing this project. What a major responsibility it is. A picture of Giotto's bell tower can be found in figure 2, while figure 3 illustrates a fifteenth-century model of the original Cathedral façade.

The elegant colored marbles that grace the bell tower were brought from quarries in the surrounding area: red from Siena, white from Carrara, and green from Prato. That in and of itself seems like it must have been a challenge, yet you know that those quarries have been in use for building materials and sculptures for some time. The men who cart the materials to the city must be very skilled, you think, as they transport their precious loads from the quarries. You ponder how they have accomplished this. Perhaps they put the materials on boats or barges and take them down to the marina at Pisa and then up the Arno. That would certainly make it easier to transport such heavy materials. You have also heard that the original physical model of the cathedral did not stand the test of time very well, and so fifty years ago the

FIGURE 2 Giotto's bell tower, contemporary view.

FIGURE 3 Model of fifteenth-century façade from the Museo del Opera.

members of the Opera del Duomo (the arm of the Arte della Lana overseeing day-to-day work, often referred to as simply the Opera), asked for new models. The winning entry by Nero di Fioravanti is spectacular looking. You stop by to admire the scale model of the finished building which is set up in one of the side aisles. It includes that dome you've been thinking about. You wonder if anyone will ever figure out how to erect that dome and finish the project.

In fact, that is the problem that everyone is discussing lately: How to construct the dome? You hear people talk about it all the time at family gatherings, at your guild, and in the cafés and piazzas. If built as designed, it will be the largest dome ever constructed. So intimidating is this task that although fifty years have passed since it was

designed and more than 100 years have gone by since construction on the church started (in 1296), no one has figured out how to do it. Can current citizens of Florence solve this problem? Would looking back to ancient examples help answer the mystery of how to build this now? Will advice from newly available works like Vitruvius's *On Architecture* be of help? What about how this project will reflect on the ability of Florentines to put their collaborative civic mechanisms to work for the good of the city? How incredible if you could see this dome rise in your lifetime. Is that a real possibility? It is true that one can look at the model and see how it uses horizontal bands of stone to resist the outward pressures of the pointed ribbed arches, but the model is made of wood. Just how someone will actually do the work on such a large

FIGURE 4 Model of cupola (dome) from the Museo del Opera, Florence.

scale is still unclear. At this point there are more questions than answers. You look forward to seeing what the different competing teams propose to solve these problems and to hearing what your fellow citizens have to say about it. No one will ever accuse your peers of lacking an opinion. You look forward to a lively discussion. You will find a model of the cupola in figure 4.

This is a heady time for you and your fellow citizens of Florence. New philosophical and practical ideas are taking root, and scholars are looking for ways to link your famously mercantile city to the glories of Rome and to the wisdom of the ancients across many fields. The aesthetics of the classical world inspire wonder. How *did they* manage to build all those famous temples and theaters, stadiums and porticos back then, without the skills that you and your fellow Florentines now possess? You have visited some ancient Roman and Greek ruins yourself, but just looking at them and walking around them doesn't always reveal just how they were made, at least not to you.

On the other hand, several crucial ancient works have only just been rediscovered and made available for study. Perhaps they hold the key to how those monuments were built. You remember the excitement throughout Florence a mere four years ago when Poggio Bracciolini, a native son, notary, and papal secretary, found a copy of Vitruvius's *On Architecture* in a dusty monastery library in the town of Saint Gallen, Switzerland. He was supposed to be at work following his duties as papal nuncio at the Council of Constance . . . but you guess even men in such a position have some free time once in a while, even in the midst of such momentous and important events. The book is very impressive. Not only does it speak of the great ancient monuments and their proportions, decorations, and settings, but it also provides information on the technologies used to build them. Perhaps someday it will be of use to contemporary builders. Perhaps anyone weighing in on questions regarding the building of the dome would be well advised to become familiar with this work.

You have had a chance to see a copy of this famed book,[4] but it leaves you with many questions. Do you have the knowledge and confidence to address questions of art, aesthetics, engineering, math, economics, politics, and philosophy? Each of these areas of knowledge seems so broad and deep, how can anyone become a master of all of them? You know that the men who design and construct the beautiful buildings in your city (and in others as well) aren't always stonecutters or bricklayers; they come from many different practical and artistic fields. You even have ideas sometimes about how work that you observe around town might be carried out more efficiently or might have fit in with its surroundings better, but you have never before had an opportunity to share your ideas with others. Of course you know that people have built magnificent meaningful buildings utilizing a wide range of skills and disciplinary ideas all through the centuries. This time it is the challenge facing you and your fellow Florentine citizens. Maybe through Florence's famous guilds an answer will emerge. They have been very much involved in the sponsoring and building of many of

Florence's most important and magnificent buildings and spaces.

Your contemporaries see no reason why guilds (also known as the *Arti* or *Corporazioni*) rather than governments cannot sponsor major civic projects and oversee their construction. Why can't artisans also understand the principles of geometry and physics? Why shouldn't all citizens have responsibilities to their city and be able to discuss and debate the merits of ideas, however challenging? This line of thought leads you to wonder what the members of the competing teams are thinking. Are they concerned about these issues too, or are they more focused on explaining what they are doing? You realize that when it comes time to hear from them, there will be many questions for them from the jury. You hope they will all be prepared to answer those questions, in addition to explaining how they will solve this puzzle.

You realize you've been lost in thought for a long time and must go back into the bright sunshine and continue to your destination. It is also time for you to immerse yourself in this way of thinking because you will have a big decision to make in the coming days as a member of the commission to select the best plan to build the dome.

HOW TO PLAY THIS GAME

This is a "reacting" game. Reacting games are complex role-playing games, used to teach about moments in history. After a few preparatory lectures, the game begins and the students are in charge. Set in moments of heightened historical tension, the games place students in the roles of historical figures. By reading the game book and their individual role sheets, students discover their objectives, potential allies, and the forces that stand between them and victory. They must then attempt to achieve victory through formal speeches, informal debate, negotiations, and (sometimes) conspiracy. Outcomes sometimes part from actual history; a postmortem session sets the record straight.

4. Originally written in approximately the first century B.C.E.

The following is an outline of what you will encounter in reacting and what you will be expected to do.

Game Setup

Your instructor will spend some time before the beginning of the game helping you to understand the historical context for the game. During the setup period, you will use several different kinds of materials:

- The game book (from which you are reading now), which includes historical information, rules and elements of the game, and essential documents.
- A role sheet provided by your instructor, which provides a short biography of the historical figure you will model in the game as well as that person's ideology, objectives, responsibilities, and resources. Your role may be an actual historical figure or a composite.

You may be required to read, in addition to the game book, historical documents or books written by historians. These provide additional information and arguments for use during the game.

Read all of this contextual material and all of these documents and sources before the game begins. And just as important, go back and reread these materials throughout the game. A second and third reading while you are in role will deepen your understanding and alter your perspective, for ideas take on a different aspect when seen through the eyes of a partisan actor.

Students who have carefully read the materials and who know the rules of the game will invariably do better than those who rely on general impressions and uncertain memories.

Game Play

Once the game begins, class sessions are presided over by students. In most cases, a single student serves as a kind of presiding officer. The instructor then becomes the Gamemaster (GM) and takes a seat in the back of the room. Though they do not lead the class sessions, GMs may do any of the following:

- Pass notes.
- Announce important events (e.g., Sparta is invading!). Some of these events are the result of student actions; others are instigated by the GM.
- Redirect proceedings that have strayed too far from the topic or activities.

The presiding officer is expected to observe basic standards of fairness, but as a fail-safe device, most reacting to the past games employ the "Podium Rule," which allows a student who has not been recognized to approach the podium and wait for a chance to speak. Once at the podium, the student has the floor and must be heard.

Role sheets contain private, secret information which students are expected to guard. You are advised, therefore, to exercise caution when discussing your role with others. Your role sheet probably identifies likely allies, but even they may not always be trustworthy. However, keeping your own counsel, or saying nothing to anyone, is not an option. In order to achieve your objectives, you *must* speak with others. You will never muster the voting strength to prevail without allies. Collaboration and coalition building are at the heart of every game.

These discussions must lead to action, which often means proposing, debating, and passing legislation. Someone therefore must be responsible for introducing the measure and explaining its particulars. And always remember that a reacting game is only a game—resistance, attack, and betrayal are not to be taken personally, since game opponents are merely acting as their roles direct.

Some games feature strong alliances called *factions*. Factions are tight-knit groups with fixed objectives. Games with factions all include roles called indeterminates. They operate outside of the established factions. Not all indeterminates are entirely neutral; some are biased on certain issues. If you are in a faction, cultivating indeterminates is in your interest, since they can be convinced to support your position. If you are lucky enough to have drawn the role of an indeterminate you should be pleased; you will likely play a pivotal role in the outcome of the game.

Game Requirements

Students in reacting games practice persuasive writing, public speaking, critical thinking, team-work, negotiation, problem solving, collaboration, adapting to changing circumstances, and working under pressure to meet deadlines. Your instructor will explain the specific requirements for your class. In general, though, a reacting game asks you to perform three distinct activities:

Reading and Writing. This standard academic work is carried on more purposefully in a reacting course, since what you read is put to immediate use, and what you write is meant to persuade others to act the way you want them to. The reading load may have slight variations from role to role; the writing requirement depends on your particular course. Papers are often policy statements, but they can also be autobiographies, battle plans, spy reports, newspapers, poems, or after-game reflections. Papers provide the foundation for the speeches delivered in class.

Public Speaking and Debate. In the course of a game, almost everyone is expected to deliver at least one formal speech from the podium (the length of the game and the size of the class will determine the number of speeches). Debate follows. Debate can be impromptu, raucous, and fast paced, and results in decisions voted on by the body. Gamemasters may stipulate that students must deliver their papers from memory when at the podium, or

may insist that students wean themselves from dependency on written notes as the game progresses.

Wherever the game imaginatively puts you, it will surely not put you in the classroom of a twenty-first-century American college. Accordingly, the colloquialisms and familiarities of today's college life are out of place. Never open your speech with a salutation like "Hi guys" when something like "Fellow citizens!" would be more appropriate.

Never be friendless when standing at the podium. Do your best to have at least one supporter second your proposal, come to your defense, or admonish inattentive members of the body. Note-passing and side conversations, while common occur-rences, will likely spoil the effect of your speech, so you and your supporters should insist upon order before such behavior becomes too disruptive. Ask the presiding officer to assist you, if necessary, and the Gamemaster as a last resort.

Strategizing. Communication among students is an essential feature of reacting games. You will find yourself writing emails, texting, attending out-of-class meetings, or gathering for meals on a fairly regular basis. The purpose of frequent communication is to lay out a strategy for advancing your agenda and thwarting the agenda of your opponents, and to hatch plots to ensnare individuals trou-bling to your cause. When communicating with a fellow student in or out of class, always assume that he or she is speaking to you in role. If you want to talk about the "real world," make that clear.

COUNTERFACTUALS

While this competition did actually take place and there was a formal announcement made for bids posted August 1418, we don't know all the details of what each proposal contained, nor who all the people were on each submission team. We do know that there were seventeen plans submitted.[5] Battista d'Antonio was in fact one of the Opera's foremen for cathedral construction, although perhaps not on the judging committee. We know a few of the names of people in Brunelleschi's and Ghiberti's groups and the list of competitors listed in footnote 5. Almost all of the characters in this game were alive during the period in question, and most are well-known citizens of Florence. That said, some were on the young side and not in the full strength of their artistic powers, and we don't have biographical information for many of the artisans, lawyers, and notaries who were involved, and although their names have been taken from historical records, their biographies have been devised based on information known about people with similar backgrounds. We do not know the names of all the people on the final jury that selected the winning proposal, and it is unlikely that all the people in this game were involved (although many may have been giving ideas and "consulting" on the side). Within the context of the game, it is important to bring out the many ideas circulating and informing the decisions that were made in the selection process, and the game reflects that. Finally, the issue of perspective is introduced in the game, but it is something that is being explored at this time. Brunelleschi's first drawings and use of the method were likely just in the experimental stage; he does not begin applying them until about two years after this, for example, in his architectural drawings for the Ospedale degli Innocenti (foundling hospital). These ideas will be expanded later still by Leon Battista Alberti.

5. Plans were submitted by "Filippo di ser Brunellescho, Manno di Bennincasa, Giovanni dell'Abbaco, Andrea di Giovanni, Giovanni di Ambrogio, Matteo di Leonardo, Lorenzo Ghiberti, Piero d'Antonio, Piero di Santa Maria a Monte, Bruno di ser Lapo, Leonarduzzo di Pier, Forzone di Nicola di Luca Spinella, Ventura di Tuccio and Matteo di Cristoforo, Bartolomeo di Jacopo, Simone di'Antonio from Siena, Michele di Nicola Dini, Giuliano d'Arrigo (Pesello)." Roberto Corazzi and Giuseppe Conti, *Il Segreto della Cupola del Brunelleschi a Firenze/The Secret of Brunelleschi's Dome in Florence* (Florence: Angelo Pontecorboli Editore, 2011), 47.

2

Historical Background

1293—The Ordinances of Justice passed. These formed the basis for the Florentine constitution through much of the Renaissance.

1296—Cathedral of Santa Maria del Fiore designed by Arnolfo di Cambio, who is said (by Vasari) to have also designed the Signoria Palace, which was the seat of Florentine government.

1304—Francesco Petrarca (known as Petrarch in many places) born in Arezzo, Italy.

1308-21—*The Divine Comedy* written by Dante Alighieri.

1313—Giovanni Boccaccio born in or near Florence, Italy.

1329—Andrea Pisano awarded the commission to create the south doors of Florence's baptistry (completed 1336).

1330—The Opera del Duomo is established by the Arte della Lana to oversee work on the Cathedral of Santa Maria del Fiore.

1331—Coluccio Salutati, scholar, humanist, political leader born in Stignano, Italy.

1348—bubonic plague (also known as the Black Death) decimates much of Europe. In the next three years between 25 percent and 50 percent of the population of Europe dies.

1358—The *Decameron*, Boccaccio's great work about the many intertwining stories of seven women and three men over a period of ten days while escaping the plague.

1370—Leonardo Bruni (statesman, historian, humanist, papal nunzio for four popes, student and mentee of Salutati) born in Arezzo, Italy.

1374—Coluccio Salutati, elected chancellor of Florence, Italy.

1377—Filippo Brunelleschi born in Florence, Italy.

1378—Lorenzo Ghiberti born in Pelago, Italy.

1378—Under pressure from the artisans, Florence undergoes constitutional reforms admitting members of the minor guilds into some government offices.

1390-92—Florence at war with Gian Galeazzo Visconti, duke of Milan; Milan held at bay.

1397—Medici Bank founded by Giovanni di Bicci de' Medici.

1397—Coluccio Salutati brings Manuel Chrysoloras to Florence to teach Greek, opening the door for many other scholars to read ancient texts in their original language.

1397-98—Florence at war with Milan. The war ended badly for Florence.

1401—Competition announced by the Arte di Calimala (Cloth Merchants, Textile Importers and Refinishers Guild) to design the north doors of baptistry. Both Ghiberti and Brunelleschi submit designs. Commission goes to Ghiberti.

1400-2—Florence at war with Milan. Outbreak of plague and attacks by Milan, followed by the death of Milan's leader, Gian Galeazzo Visconti. The latter leaves Florence free of the threat of Milan.

1410—Leonardo Bruni elected chancellor of Florence.

1414—(November 5)-1418 (April 22) Council of Constance. At this historic gathering, church leaders addressed (1) the extinction of the so-called Western Schism; (2) the reformation of ecclesiastical government and life; (3) the repression of heresy; (4) attendance at the council; general considerations. At the end, Pope Martin V is formally recognized as pope. One of his first stops will be in Florence.

1418—August 18 announcement of the competition for the commission to construct the dome of the Cathedral of Santa Maria del Fiore.

NARRATIVE

The city of Florence sits inland among rolling hills along the River Arno. It is a thriving merchant republic. It is a small but relatively powerful independent city-state. At this time Italy as we know it did not exist, and the territory that now constitutes the country was made up of many city-states. Some of them, like Genova and Milan, were under the leadership of powerful noblemen; others, like Rome and its surrounding territory, were under the control of the pope. South of that was the Kingdom of Naples, which at this time included all of the territory of southern Italy and Sicily. At this moment it is ruled by Angevin nobility (from France). Florence, with its republican form of government and rotating sets of elected leaders, represented a rather novel form of government, one that the citizens were very proud of saying made them the heirs of the Roman republic—which was a very powerful idea to their citizens despite the fact that political power was contested by wealthy families and powerful guilds and church leaders.

Construction on the Cathedral of Santa Maria del Fiore started during what we refer to today as the High Middle Ages in 1296. It was designed in 1296 by Arnolfo di Cambio in the Gothic style,[1] but once building was underway (rising on the site of a former church, Santa Reparata), plans were altered. As building proceeded, those overseeing the project had a change of heart, preferring a more roman style[2] that included an octagonal drum from which a great dome would rise. Di Cambio, having died only a few years after the construction of his church had begun, was not in a position to protest any changes. In 1331 members of the Arte della Lana (Wool Guild) who were overseeing the construction put the well-respected painter Giotto in charge of construction, and he oversaw the construction of the church's magnificent bell tower.

Over the succeeding 122 years many things happened, both in the world at large and in Florence. Dante Alighieri published his great work *The Divine Comedy*, and he did so in Italian, opening the world of ideas and literature to a wider audience. Instead of appealing only to the scholarly intellectuals who read Latin, Dante wrote his

---

1. This style was first developed in France, but there are examples from Florence such as the Church of Santa Maria Novella.

2. An example of this earlier style, often called Romanesque in English, is the Church of Santi Apostoli in Florence, which you might find in an internet search.

great poem in the language of the people. His example was followed by other great Florentine writers such as Francesco Petrarca and Giovanni Boccaccio. What is more, they wrote on subjects that spoke to knowledge not only of the past but also of the present. Boccaccio even based his inventive stories on events of the relatively contemporary bubonic plague which so decimated the population of Europe that it changed the economic and intellectual landscape as people succumbed to the epidemic.

As Florence regained its feet after the human destruction brought about by the plague (also called the Black Death), its social, economic, political, and intellectual life flowered anew, influenced by the ideas of people like Petrarch and Boccaccio and in part by its unusual form of government, a republic governed in large part by elected members of its major guilds. Leadership positions were kept only for a few months, and while such constant shifts in leadership may seem excessive to us today, the idea was to keep any one person or group from amassing the power to take over (at least for a while). This might be understood as a form of constraint on the consolidation of power. By the time of our game, however, the government structure has shifted to include more citizens, thus diminishing the power of the guilds to some extent. That said, many citizens were members of guilds and officeholders in guilds as well as prominent citizens in their neighborhoods. Opening up the city's leadership to people elected by neighborhood (still keeping to short revolving terms of service) was meant to reflect new, more inclusive ideas of leadership for the city.

The game takes place in the spring and summer of 1418. It is hot and muggy, and Firenze (Florence) is a prosperous city of nearly 40,000. The River Arno provides it with an important means for transporting goods and contributes to the city's position as a major commercial center in Tuscany, where many contemporary cities had fewer than 10,000 inhabitants. It is a lovely, powerful city that is also very proud of itself and its achievements.

Some say its citizens are haughty or arrogant. Florentines don't give much credence to those people. They are proud of their illustrious native sons, the writers and artists mentioned in the sections above but also artists such as Donato di Niccolò di Betto Bardi (known as Donatello), Paolo Ucello, Nanni di Banco, Lorenzo Ghiberti, and Filippo Brunelleschi. There are also many influential and wealthy families who vie for recognition and power. These families include bankers and merchants such as the Strozzi, Medici, Albizzi, Ridolfi, Aldobrandini, Pitti, Ricasoli, and Pazzi. They are in a position to influence the city through the political offices they rotate in and out of and by using their wealth to commission private and public projects that keep many of the creative citizens of the city busy.

Merchants and scholars of the city have taken great pains to illuminate anyone who will listen to them about Florence's unique place as a city founded on independent principles that stretch back to Rome's republican ideals. Both Coluccio Salutati and Leonardo Bruni have written important histories of the city. You should become more familiar with some of their works (see Texts section). Florentines are also immensely proud of the beauty of their city, whose praises have been sung by Dante, this despite his having been exiled from his beloved city, although he was returning to a much-favored native son status by the time of our game. Perhaps his attitude and his words will be of inspiration to students in playing this game, as they have been to many a Florentine citizen.

San Giovanni Battista (St John the Baptist) is the city's patron saint. His feast day is June 24, and this is a very important yearly civic and religious event. His protection and guidance are sought for the benefit of the city and its citizens particularly on his feast day, which is celebrated with much pomp even in the present day.

Early in the 1400s, humanism took root in the urban setting of Florence, from whence it spread to other areas of Italy. One of the first works published proposing the new concepts that tie a reverence for the past to the pride in the intellectual and creative work of current citizens as more than just the spark of the divine was *De Ingenuis Moribus et Liberalibus Studiis* (On Noble Manners and Liberal Studies) written by Petrus Paulus Vergerius. His treatise appeared a little over a decade before the start of the game in 1402–3 (see excerpts in the Core Texts section or full text online).[3] Vergerius laid out the basic ideas that formed the foundation of humanist thought and that continued to be developed by other people. He illustrated the point that the achievements and goals of society should be seen as rooted in human endeavor and not dependent on the divine, and thus educating young people in a broad range of subjects would aid in the development of good citizens and neighbors. In looking for methods to attain this, he touted a system whereby individuals would cultivate the necessary skills through humanistic studies. The thinking was that those who were exposed to these foundational subjects which today we associate with the liberal arts would become valued and admired leaders of society. They might not all agree, but the process of thinking and approaching problems was shared as was the importance of certain fundamental ideas. As Florence grew and became an important political and cultural player in the Italian peninsula, this development meant that the subjects of grammar, rhetoric, poetry, history, and moral philosophy were put front and center as the foundations of learning and humanistic thought. They were considered vital to developing an informed citizenship, citizens who would take part in government and make civic decisions that affect all citizens. These are the ideas that you should use in your papers and presentations and to support your choice of proposal if on the jury or in developing your proposal if you are on one of the teams.

There are many other illustrious scholars in addition to Vergerius as well as notaries and political figures of importance who have helped to establish the new ideas of humanism in Florence, men such as Coluccio Salutati, Leonardo Bruni, and Poggio Bracciolini. These scholars and others were looking for ways to acknowledge the many incredible contributions to philosophy, math, art, music, and other areas of human endeavor that people developed rather than claiming that everything good was due directly to destiny. In addition, these thinkers believed their ideas had deep roots because they saw the foundation of those ideas in the ancient past. In fact, the Florentines were especially keen to stake a claim to their classical and republican Roman inheritance, priding themselves on creating a city and civic structure that owed much to ideas first proposed in the ancient world. This is an important aspect of the new ways of thinking. Of course, if more weight is given to the achievements of humans, so too must their ethical and moral responsibilities grow. Florentines, who are very proud of their government, see these ideas as a way of legitimizing their republic, and they look for opportunities to make the connection to the power of ancient republican Rome. Sometimes that may have just meant taking visitors through the streets by way of the old Roman walls (which were no longer standing, but the streets followed their outline), although the major Roman streets passing by the old forum (now the market square) were still there. For Florentines this urban design shows the city's continuity with the greatness that was Rome. The focus on incorporating the benefits of philosophy, the arts, math, and astronomy into a way of reasoning and interacting with the world also found its roots in the past but would now be developed in the next 200 years in a robust manner for educating people to engage in the world that is still important in contemporary times.

Florentines were extremely proud of the fact that they were citizens living in a city with an elected leader rather than a hereditary lord like the citizens living in Milan, who were under the thumb of the feared Visconti family. It must be said, of

3. Hanover Historical Texts Project.

course, that until sixteen years ago (game time), Florence was also in fear of the duke of Milan. Giangaleazzo Visconti was a ruthless man intent on bringing Florence under his control, and the city was not unhappy when he passed away. In the intervening years the city prospered and grew in many ways, including by going to war with neighboring communities to bring them under Florence's control. This happened to the city of Arezzo, and the desire for a port led to wars with Pisa as well. Of course, while there are Florentines who liked the excitement of battle and others who were of a more intellectual bent, there were many Florentine citizens who did not think so well of those scholars and pious men who had withdrawn from the public arena. In their view, what a good society needs are active citizens.

One of the most important aspects of this relatively new way of approaching life was its moral underpinnings. The belief was that the kind of education promoted by these humanists could make you a responsible parent, colleague, and citizen and prepare one for life whether as a head of household, teacher, or civil servant. But the ideals of humanism do more than prepare a person for that person's chores in life; they open the way for analysis and a critical awareness of existing values (skills that we still value). Additionally, they were seen to lead to an examination and exploration of past societies in light of these new ideals. This, in turn, allowed a person to apply those newfound ideas to that person's own time and place with respect to both human behavior and the surrounding physical environment. For some people living in Florence at this time, this intellectual challenge gave life in Florence its special quality and inspired the way they worked to beautify and expand their city. As a citizen in this world, you will be applying the ideas expressed by Vergerius, Bruni, and the other authors you explore by infusing their ideas into what you say and write as your character. You will consider not only whether the proposals presented do the job, but whether they bridge this

link to the past, whether the scale of the project is in keeping with the city's historical past and its desired future.

Architecture, like literature, paintings, or sculpture, can represent intellectual ideals. Buildings and piazzas, arches and fountains can reflect the grand humanistic view of the world. In fact, contributing to the urban landscape has roots in republican Roman ideas, where it was seen as a civic duty for senators and other leaders to give back to their communities by building theaters, temples, circuses, and other public works. This habit can be seen in Florence as well, where wealthy merchants built chapels and contributed to the finances of public works and where guilds took on the responsibilities of funding and overseeing the construction of churches, hospitals, and other public buildings.

It was also believed that Florence must grow and prosper because that is good for all of its citizens. That said, there are many competing families and associations, guilds, and even churches. It might be difficult to imagine how they managed to work together and not just for their own ends. One way to do this was to keep front and center that what was good for Florence needed to come first. This was particularly reinforced when the guilds elected councils and government leaders to administer the city. At the time of our game, participation has expanded to include a greater number of Florentines, something that Leonardo Bruni advocated, but the old maxim "That which touches all must be approved by all" was still a guiding principle if you wanted to govern this city or successfully direct projects here.[4] It would be prudent to keep this idea in mind during the game.

This view of the informed citizen also applies to the merchant citizens of Florence who prized travel

4. John Najemy, "Guild Republicanism in Trecento Florence: The Successes and Ultimate Failure of Corporate Politics," *American Historical Review* 84, no. 1 (February 1979): 65.

and international connections. As the merchant Goro Dati wrote, "A Florentine who is not a merchant, who has not traveled the world over, seeing foreign nations and peoples before returning to Florence with riches, is a man who deserves no esteem whatsoever."[5] Within the game students will need to demonstrate how "worldly" and well informed they are. One way this can be done (where appropriate) is to make comparisons with other places that your character might have visited and utilizing that knowledge to illustrate how travel can inform choices made at home.

The ruins of the great cities of the Greek and Roman world influenced the aesthetics and ideas of Florentine citizens. While most people didn't travel all that far, many people would have been familiar with the Roman ruins in Rome, Milan, and other Tuscan cities. Some perhaps would also know some of the Roman remains in places as far away as France—bridges such as the Ponte du Gard, or amphitheaters such as the one in Arles. Perhaps someone may have traveled as far as Paestum, located south of Naples. This was a foreign land then under the control of Joanna (Giovanna) II of Anjou. If they had gone to Paestum, they would have visited the magnificent Greek temples there, but most people would have had knowledge of things within the region of Tuscany. Artists of all kinds regularly visited at least the closer monuments. The fallen columns, sculptures, and architecture of the ancient world represented (and still represent) amazing feats of engineering and deep aesthetic beauty. Some artists went to visit them with the aim of understanding how the monuments were made. This they did by carefully sketching and measuring the ruins and trying to understand how weight was distributed. In some cases, they then went home to experiment on their own to test their understanding.

Donatello did this, for example, after observing hollow statues made using the lost wax technique.[6] As a result, the remains of these ancient cities were deeply influential on the art and architecture of the day. This is particularly true in Florence.

This is an exciting time in terms of learning because many disciplines are being enriched by the rediscovery of the ancient texts written by Greek and Roman authors. There were also texts coming to light written by Islamic scholars who had preserved many earlier Greek texts by translating them while also building upon that earlier knowledge when working in academies founded in Sicily and other areas of Italy. All these texts that were now appearing drove some Florentine citizens (and others) to visit monastic libraries with the express purpose of looking for texts that no one had paid much attention to or that people were unsure existed. One might even say that for some, this activity had become a form of intellectual treasure hunt driven by curiosity, as they searched out works that were mentioned as existing in "ancient days." When new works were found and then translated, they excited discussion and debate among intellectuals whether they were academics, clergy, or common citizens. These sleuths were driven by the power of the ideas they had seen referred to in the works they did know but perhaps thought the originals were lost forever. Perhaps they will be inspirational to you as well.

The study of all of these subjects was thought to help develop the attributes that make men and women human. Some people, such as the notary Poggio Bracciolini, traveled a great deal. In his case it was due to his work for the city and for the

5. Stefano Ugo Baldassarri and Arielle Saiber, eds., *Images of Quattrocento Florence: Selected Writings in Literature, History, and Art* (New Haven, Conn.: Yale University Press, 2000), xxiii.

6. In this process, a wax model is made and covered with a clay mold. The hot metal is then poured into the mold to melt the wax, which exits through a hole in the bottom. Once cooled, the mold is opened to reveal the item cast. It is also possible to do this with a heat-resistant core within the wax, resulting in a metal object with a hollow core.

church as a papal nunzio. He seems to have spent a great deal of his free time hunting for lost manuscripts. Among his most recent was his rediscovery in 1417 of Lucretius's text *De rerum natura* (On the Nature of Things). He worked feverishly on a transcription, but it took time to write it all out in his famously beautiful script. Those who heard of it reported it to be scandalous.

Four years prior to the start of our game, in 1414, while taking time off from his work at the Council of Constance, Bracciolini was searching in an abbey in Saint Gallen, Switzerland, when he made one of his most remarkable discoveries. Among the musty works was a copy of *De Architectura* (On Architecture) by the great Roman architect Vitruvius. This find stimulated people like Brunelleschi and Donatello. It is said that after having read this work, they visited the original Roman buildings and were then inspired to measure and draw them in order to learn how they were constructed. Now, finally, some light might be shed on the construction of some of the most famous works of antiquity. Or so it was hoped. Many different aspects of Florentine life have contributed to the development of these new ideas, and they have influenced commerce, government, construction, architecture, and the arts.

Who are the men who will confront this massive undertaking of completing the dome and thus the church? To the patricians of Florentine society, they are perhaps simply "engineers," certainly not artists, and yet to the humanist scholars there should not be such a distinction. In their minds there *are* people who possess the capacity for invention and originality that are as important to creation as they are mysterious to understand.[7] Most of the men who will compete for the contract to construct the dome will not possess a university education. Most will have learned their skills through apprenticeships in a process of watching

and imitating the master.[8] To many Florentines these practical ways of working are of course important, but they cannot be placed on the same level as intellectual inquiry. Is this a real conflict or simply a question of not understanding how ideas about book learning and practical experience can come together? Is this a simple issue of being open to how invention and artistry can mesh with hands-on skills and high aesthetics? Perhaps in the construction of the dome there may be a chance to appreciate the deep knowledge, invention, and creativity and thus to elevate those in the mechanical arts.

The City

Florence's prosperous mercantile classes and its governing structure play particularly important roles in city life. Florentine merchants have plied their trade far and wide for many generations. Wool and silk processing and manufacturing in particular have made many quite rich. But this is also a city of factions and political rivalries with its own very unusual form of government. The city is divided into four districts known to the inhabitants as *quartieri*. Each one is named for an important church—Santo Spirito, Santa Croce, Santa Maria Novella, and San Giovanni.[9] Each *quartieri* has its own *gonfalone* (standard or flag) with its own symbol, and the person who carries it is called the *Gonfaloniere*. This person is the head of that district, or in the case of officials elected to administer the city, the chief civil magistrate (in other words, there are four neighborhoods, each with a flag and set of symbols and a leader for each neighborhood plus leaders of the city as a whole).

7. Christine Smith, *Architecture in the Culture of Early Humanism: Ethics, Aesthetics, and Eloquence, 1400–1470* (New York: Oxford University Press, 1991), 30.

8. Tim Ingold, *Making: Anthropology, Archaeology, Art and Architecture* (London: Routledge, 2013), 52.

9. Goro Dati, "The Structure of the Florentine Government," in *Images of Quattrocento Florence: Selected Writings in Literature, History, and Art*, ed. Stefano Ugo Baldassarri and Arielle Saiber (New Haven, Conn.: Yale University Press, 2000), 45.

Nearly all Florentine citizens belong to one of its twenty-one powerful *Corporazioni*, referred to by name as the *Arti* (guilds—see list below). These are divided into the Major and Minor Arts. They are professional associations that have specific expectations with regard to duties and behaviors of their members and admission requirements. Each guild has a leader or *priori*, and there are two of these for every district who are in charge of administering justice under the Standard Bearer of Justice. Each district elects someone to this position from among those men who are forty years old or older.[10] This structure illustrates how civic responsibility is woven into people's everyday activities. Members of the guilds thus have duties within the guilds but also represent their professions and their neighborhoods in administering justice within the city. There are very strict rules about the Standard Bearer of Justice and other administrative offices, each of which lasts for terms of two months. During the period that a person holds one of these administrative offices, the officials leave their homes and live in the government palace, the Palazzo della Signoria, where they eat, sleep and govern during their two months in office (for further details, see Goro Dati's full description in the text in chapter 5). It may seem irrational that officeholders must move away from home while they hold office, but the idea was to keep people accountable by having the leaders all together in the place where they governed, thus preventing corruption. On the other hand, no one would leave their families for too long, so it was a quickly rotating office (this was also thought to help keep corruption down).

As you can see, this was a very regulated and organized city, and its citizens were extremely confident in their unique method of managing their affairs. This method influenced all aspects of Florentine life. As with any city and any time period, people had many roles in life. They held office, and then left office to return to civic life. They belonged to many organizations. They might have led some of them. This meant that within any organization, individuals would want what was best for the organization, but they would also keep in mind how decisions affected them in the other areas of their lives and with regard to the other people they dealt with. At this time, the power of the guilds to govern Florence was diminishing. They still had a strong public influence in terms of public works, sponsoring the construction of the churches, hospitals, and other civic works, but governing was passing to a broader electorate. Some folks would have found this difficult to accept. Some families, like those of the Strozzi, Pazzi, Albizzi, and Medici, were becoming more wealthy and prominent and itching for more power. Some citizens were concerned that these families could have unbalanced the existing power structure, but the push to include more citizens in the city's administration had been strong and the guilds hadn't lost all their power by any means. In fact, major projects, like the construction of the Cathedral of Santa Maria del Fiore, were a testament to both the older guild government system and the effects of the new broader electorate. Whatever happens in our game, everyone involved must see this project through to the end, or the crowning glory of the city will instead be an embarrassment that rival cities will capitalize on.

Architecture

While none of the individuals involved with the design and construction of Florence's public buildings were technically architects or engineers, people have been constructing monumental buildings, simple habitations, religious structures, bridges, and other public spaces since antiquity. Using basic tools such as saws and molds, chisels and axes, cords and wheels, pulleys and levers, people have erected an amazing range of structures. In the classical Greek world, choosing the place to situate a religious or public building was critical to

10. Dati, "Structure of Florentine Government," 46.

its success. The designers would take into consideration not only the plot being built on but also how people would approach the area and practice their rituals. Temples were the homes of the gods or the gods and the priests who tended to them, and the rituals and festivities took place in the areas in front of and around the building and its porticos.

In the Roman world, thinking about how the space would be used continued to resonate. The Romans continued to play with the earlier ideas and to expand on ways to cover large spaces imbuing their architecture with their own worldview. How Romans (and others since) designed and organized outdoor and indoor spaces was a reflection of their worldview, their community, their communal activities, and their values. Each space can be seen a reflection of the activities within and the needs of the community (how many people will it hold, what kinds of hierarchies in terms of duties and activities, how egalitarian or not, and so on).[11] By the mid-imperial period, Romans had mastered the design of curved spaces using arches and groined and barrel vaults to help lift the ceiling higher and to cover large spaces. With time, they learned that these features could exist in the building without being seen. That is, you could hide structural elements—like arches—to help distribute weight within the wall, covered with a pretty surface of lighter materials that gave texture, strength, and aesthetic design to the buildings[12] (check out the picture of Pont du Gard or the image of the Colosseum in the appendix, or search for images of them online). Anyone visiting these buildings would see the outer workings; only those with a deep interest in the engineering and construction techniques would try to work out how the pieces all came together. Children get some idea of how these things work when they build with wooden block sets that include arched pieces. One

can also examine images of Roman baths or aqueducts to get some idea of how structures are made stable. Vitruvius notes at the beginning of his treatise that builders need to be very broadly educated, or else they will not be able to see the full scope of the building or see through its execution. One needs to know not only how to build, but how the building will be used, how it will fit in with the views of those building it. You can see that this is one of those basic concepts that gets adapted and expanded by the humanist thinkers.

All workers would have had access to rulers, T squares, compasses, and plumb bobs (a line with a pointy weight that you can use to ascertain that something is in vertical alignment). Basic line levels with oil and water in a tube or cup can be used to make sure things are horizontally level. Levers of various sorts can be used to heave up very heavy weights, and these can be transported with relative ease if placed on a few iron or wood rollers. The heavy weight is pushed across the rollers, and then when the last roller is exposed, it is taken and brought to the front. Molds of different sizes and shapes were used to make bricks of uniform shape or to act as a measure for other materials (like checking to see if your carry-on luggage is of regulation size by seeing if it will fit in the frame provided at the airport). Romans also had the use of concrete (this is a mix of mortar, often pozzolana [a coarse volcanic stone with high silica content], river gravel, and bits and pieces of rocks, old bricks or building stones, etc.). It could also be used to create a wall (by building a frame and filling it with the concrete and removing the frame once the inside had set) that would later be faced with other, more attractive materials using less of those precious materials in the building process.

Other basic equipment that people used included wooden cranes (basically a wooden stand built as a kind of A frame braced by cords). The two uprights hold a pulley wheel between them, and a cord runs from a round bar or dowel, which is the

11. Frank Edward Brown, *Roman Architecture* (New York: George Braziller, 1976).

12. Brown, *Roman Architecture*.

crossbar of the A frame, and over the wheel and is attached to the thing you want to lift. The bar with the cord has an X handle on each side that can be turned to raise the weight. If the loads are very heavy, a contraption can be constructed with a vertical pole with an X bar going through it that can be turned by four people walking in a circle, or if really large by an animal walking in a circle. That vertical pole has a cog with teeth at the top that intersects with a cog that ends in a bar that lies horizontally and whose far end might be inserted into a pulley or a wheel with containers like a Ferris wheel. By walking in a circle one can pull things up, and by reversing direction, let them down. While descriptions of traditional construction tools may be hard to understand, there are examples of them to be found in artworks that can help you visualize how they look or work. Construction methods are depicted on Trajan's column and from a slightly later period than our game, in Pieter Breughel's painting *The Tower of Babel*. You might look up these images and might also look up the panels from Giotto's bell tower for Santa Maria del Fiore. There, works by Andrea and Nicola Pisano and Luca della Robbia, among others, combine biblical images with images from the humanistic "vocabulary" including grammar and dialectic, sculpture and geometry, among others. In them you can find many of the tools that people used to design and construct things.

During the Medieval period, architecture changed its aesthetic to pointed arches rather than rounded ones. This style is referred to as gothic, and the building shapes still come down to basic geometric forms. These buildings radiate a feeling of lightness not seen in earlier buildings. There are also larger, more expansive windows. In order to build this way, there needed to be a new kind of support system. Now the pressure from the vaults can't be fully sustained by the new, slender columns. This was resolved by building buttresses, walls that act as supports, sit outside of the chapels or nave, and press inward, taking most of the weight of the building. Because they are on the outside, the inside is now freed up, giving the feeling of openness and space. Where the arches and vaults were extremely slender and tall in the interior, additional arched buttresses were added to the outside to press in and support the more simple buttresses. These arched features were called flying buttresses. For an example, search for images of the Cathedral of Notre-Dame in Paris, or even the National Cathedral in Washington, D.C. To find out more about building equipment or the building of cathedrals, you might consult David Macaulay's books *How Things Work* and *Cathedral*.

Guilds

Starting in the 1200s, guilds came to take on an ever more important role in Italian society. This was especially true of Florence. The guilds were independent organizations that formed as a way to look after the interests of people who shared a trade or business against potential exploitation from other citizens or citizen groups. What made them interesting was that unlike modern unions, they were not simply a way for workers to obtain rights from employers, but rather they were made up of people with shared interests and of mixed social class and background. That said, they did function (at least sometimes) as a collective way of pushing back on the powerful and noble families (although they might be guild members too) that represented the majority of people in high public office.

Another particularly interesting aspect of the guilds was their internal governing structure of elected officials that held office for short terms, rather like the larger civic system. In some of the guilds members took yearly oaths to uphold the values of that group, and in others they did so when assuming office. Sometimes those oaths bound them to help members of their guild who were down on their luck or otherwise in need. That might have included gathering money for widows, or arranging a loan or funds for burials and masses. Guilds set wages and prices and provided quality control.

The guilds provided a sense of shared security and a place to organize political strength among people of varied backgrounds including the artisans, notaries, merchants, and other professionals of the day. In the middle 1300s, guilds were deeply embedded into the structure of Florence's republican government, with representatives from each of the guilds sitting on the city council and taking turns in key leadership positions. By 1418, this was no longer exclusively the case, as mentioned above, but the vestiges of that manner of cooperative and communal government still existed. The possibility to partake in government had just recently been expanded to include a wider range of people. By this time, the Arte della Lana was carrying out its responsibilities for a civic project by overseeing what was essentially a public work. Some funding came from donations to the guild, but mostly it came from the Florentine government, which had given the Opera del Duomo full responsibility for overseeing the construction of the church and the dome (and some other city projects as well).[13]

Guilds were responsible for overseeing the usage of many of the city's public buildings from their construction to their maintenance. For example, the Baptistry of San Giovanni right across the plaza from the rising Santa Maria del Fiore was entrusted to the Arte di Calimala (Merchants). That was in addition to their work at the Basilica of San Miniato. Florence's three hospitals (San Marco, the Spedale degli Innocenti, and that of San Mateo and San Gallo) had construction and upkeep provided by the Arte della Seta (Silk Workers), but not all of the time. The hospital of San Mateo and San Gallo rotated to the authorities of different guilds. One final example would be the responsibilities for the hospital of San Paolo and of the Palazzo of the Tribunale di Mercantanzia and of the Basilica of Santa Croce by the Arte dei Guidici e Notai (Judges and Notaries).[14] These shifting responsibilities would have meant that a certain amount of cooperation was necessary if work was ever to get done and flow smoothly. These choices illustrate how the humanistic world view of the Florentines was put into practice.

When the work on Santa Maria del Fiore began, there were representatives of various guilds on the Opera, until it finally became the full responsibility of the Arte della Lana. During the period of our game, the Opera rarely worked totally independently. Any time major decisions needed to be made regarding the strategies for construction, or the design of the building over its 100-plus-year history, competitions would be held and commissions would be set up with representatives from different guilds and with city leaders, and there would even be open days for citizens to come and look at models and comment (perhaps a precursor to our town hall meetings on topics of public concern). Sometimes multiple meetings over months would ensue. Usually, the committees would combine features they liked from different entries and would ask the designer of the project they liked the best to alter or incorporate ideas from other entries. In this way, all project decisions reflected both the humanistic ideals of the city and its deeply held republican values.[15] Remember that quote (in the narrative section above) about how things that affect everyone must have input from everyone. You should keep this process and these ideas in mind as you maneuver in the game to achieve your goals.

13. Margaret Haines, "Brunelleschi and Bureaucracy: The Tradition of Public Patronage at the Florentine Cathedral," *I Tatti Studies in the Italian Renaissance* 3 (1989): 90–93.

14. Giovanni Fanelli and Michele Fanelli, *Brunelleschi's Cupola: Past and Present of an Architectural Masterpiece* (Florence: Mandragora, 2004), 13.

15. Fanelli and Fanelli, *Brunelleschi's Cupola*, 13.

The many and varied guilds listed below give you an idea of how professional and craft activities were sorted within the overall system. The major guilds were, like their name implies, more important in terms of the power they wielded in the civic life of Florence. To be a member of one of those *Arti* was to be a person of importance within the city's social and political structure. That said, it is conceivable that within any one extended family, members might belong to different guilds.

To join a guild, you needed to be the legitimate son of a member, demonstrate proficiency in the craft or profession in question, make a perfect example of your work, and pay a tax. Artists of various sorts were members of different sorts of guilds. Painters, for example, were members of the Arte dei Medici e Speziali, while goldsmiths were members of the Silk Guild. All guilds would also have had accountants, notaries, and lawyers to serve the guild's needs.

With regard to the Arte della Lana and the Opera, the latter was made up of four laborers who were in charge of finances, a treasurer (*camarlingo*), a notary (acting as a secretary keeping records of what was decided), and a director (for a total of seven people).[16] Members of the guild served in these roles for only two months at a time, and then rotated out. As with the rules for Florentine government as a whole, this was meant to control corruption. In a way, the guilds reflected the community's civic and political republican values on a smaller scale.

Major Guilds: judges and notaries, merchants, moneychangers, wool, silk, apothecaries and doctors, leather and fur

Minor Guilds: butchers, shoemakers, blacksmiths, stone and wood workers, linen, rag pickers, wine sellers, hotel owners, oil sellers and deli, leather and armor and swords, wood, carpenters, and bakers.

Each guild has its own crest. A selection of guilds along with illustrative crests can be found in table 1.

Feasts and Festivals

The Italian calendar, then as now, assigns a saint to every day of the year. These days are celebrated on a personal level as Name Days (i.e., you celebrate the day of the saint whose name you carry rather than your birthday) or on a civic level with city-wide festivals. These can commemorate religious holidays or the patron saint of a particular parish or city. The Festa di San Giovanni is a very important celebration in Florence. This is a major event in the city's yearly cultural and religious cycle. The festivities, which take place over several days, include markets where Florence's famous merchant classes displayed their wares. There were opportunities for the city's citizens to promenade in the streets and show their own wealth and prestige through the elegant and prestigious fabrics of their clothing and headdresses and the jewels that adorned them. But this was also a religious ceremony, one that brought together the clergy, government officials, and ordinary citizens to thank the Lord for the prosperity of their city. It was an opportunity to make vows, make donations to the church, and appear (at least at this moment) humble in front of the Lord.

It was a tradition that everyone over age fifteen carried a candle in the procession through town to the Baptistry of San Giovanni located right across the piazza from the Cathedral of Santa Maria del Fiore. As we have mentioned, every citizen held multiple roles or positions in society. A single person could thus belong to several groups; a person might belong to neighborhood groups, guilds, churches, and political or civic groups all at the same time. As a student you may find this idea challenging, but this is still a fact of life; we all have multiple and at times overlapping roles in our daily lives. The key, as always, is to juggle those responsibilities.

16. Roberto Corazzi and Giuseppe Conti, *Il Segreto della Cupola del Brunelleschi a Firenze/The Secret of Brunelleschi's Dome in Florence* (Florence: Angelo Pontecorboli Editore, 2011), 35.

TABLE 1 List of Arti and their crests

Major Guild	Guild	Crest
1. Arte dei Giudici e Notai	Judges and Notaries	
2. Arte dei Calimala	Cloth Merchants, Textile Importers, and Refinishers	
3. Arte del Cambio	Moneychangers and Bankers	
4. Arte della Lana	Wool Workers	
5. Arte della Seta	Silk Workers	
6. Arte dei Medici e Speziali	Doctors and Pharmacists	
7. Arte dei Vaiai e Pellicciai	Lace and Fur Workers	

(*continued*)

TABLE 1 (*continued*)

Minor Guild	Guild	Crest
8. Arte dei Maestri di Pietra e di Legname	Stone and Wood Workers	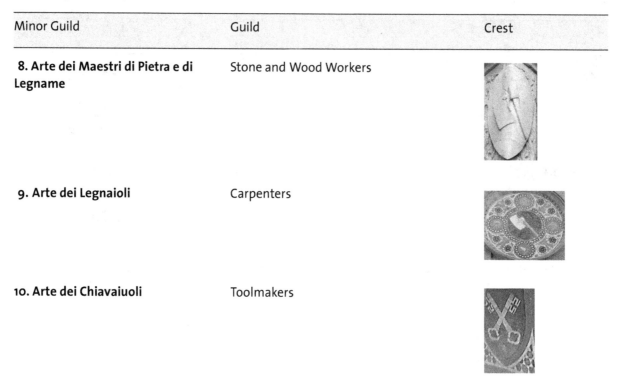
9. Arte dei Legnaioli	Carpenters	
10. Arte dei Chiavaiuoli	Toolmakers	

The festivities connected with the feast were organized by *quartieri*. Each *quartieri* and each *arte* had its own *gonfalone* (see section above), a banner hanging from a long pole that was carried by the leader of its group. On special occasions (such as the Festa di San Giovanni), a second type of banner called a *palio* was created. This vertical flag was often awarded as a prize for a sports competition held in conjunction with the religious ceremonies (for example, in the present day, a *palio* is the prize given to the winner in the twice-yearly horse races held in the main piazza of Siena, giving the event its name). The procession of the Festa di San Giovanni is headed by priests who are followed by the *gonfalone* bearer. Behind each *gonfalone* walk the leaders of the *quartieri* and those of the *arti* with their emblems of office, drummers, flag jugglers, pages, and citizens. (See images below for two examples of artworks that illustrate the procession and the *palios*. *Remember that artworks are also texts that are full of information for you to use.*)

The creation of the most beautiful *palio* was a highly contested honor. Each group wanted to create the most admired banner. This was a day for the townspeople of Florence to come out and flaunt their wares and their wealth (not to mention their beautiful women dressed to show off all that wealth). People gathered on the streets, where they watched the procession, or they marched with their group, and they ate at feasts together in the streets as a neighborhood lining the streets with long trestle tables. Of course, one can't flaunt their riches too much—that would be unseemly—

so one would also be sure to go to church and pay one's respects at mass in a more decorous way.

The Cathedral of Santa Maria del Fiore

Florence's management system also meant that the *corporazioni* had quite a bit of influence and power within the city and that they were responsible for many civic projects. The Arte della Lana (the Wool Guild), one of the city's most powerful groups, had taken responsibility for the city's most imposing project. They are the power and organization behind the construction of the magnificent Cathedral of Santa Maria del Fiore. Since 1330 the Opera del Duomo (a subgroup of the guild that was charged with administering the construction project) has been overseen by the Arte della Lana. (Take note: these men are not architects or engineers—or not necessarily!) Work on the cathedral has been a long and arduous project interrupted innumerable times by wars and plague, but the project inches forward (see image of the façade and bell tower in chapter 1) for an idea of the external particulars).

In the later 1300s adjustments to the original design were made and a beautiful, if challenging, design for the dome was created. According to the model (see image in chapter 1), the dome will sit on an octagonal drum (the foundational ring of stones from which the actual dome rises) and rise to form eight pointed arches (an arch of this sort is known as a *quinto arcuto*, defined as "an arc of radius equal to four-fifths of the dome's interior base diameter." Thus with a span of roughly 45 meters, that means that four-fifths of it would be 36 meters—see figure 5, not in scale).[17]

Fioravanti's model used rings like those around a barrel[18] (to some this may recall Dante's nine rings of Hell in the first book of his masterwork *The Divine Comedy*) so the stress would not really go into ground but would be absorbed by the whole building itself (or so it is claimed). How one would keep the pressure distributed so that it would do this is one of the challenges for whoever will build the dome. The proposed dome needs to be 72 braccia (diameter 143"6"—1 braccia is about 1.9 feet). That would make it larger than the Pantheon in Rome (see figure 6), or the Church of Hagia Sofia in Constantinople (see figure 7; in fact the diameter is roughly 1.5 contemporary basketball courts).

At the outset, when the design was first proposed, the Opera del Duomo was so worried about accepting this extravagant plan that in 1367, the guild members did what any self-respecting Florentine would do: they put the responsibility of accepting it to a vote by the citizens of Florence. It passed. This is a complicated structure. The drum's octagonal shape certainly makes the construction of the dome a challenging geometric puzzle as you can see in figure 8.[19]

Construction Challenges

In a period before electricity, building monumental structures was quite the challenge, and yet, as we see if we look around the world from 3000 B.C. or so onward, people have been able to quarry large blocks of stone, move them great distances, place them with great care (with or without mortar), and hoist them reasonably high up in the air. Look at the images at the end of the appendix or in other files your professor may provide. *All* of those buildings were built quite literally, by hand. Very impressive, when you think about it. You might wonder how they did it. There are many answers to that question, and that is part of your

17. Barry Jones, Andrea Sereni, and Massimo Ricci, "Building Brunelleschi's Dome: A Practical Methodology Verified by Experiment," *Journal of the Society of Architectural Historians* 69, no. 1 (2010): 44.

18. Jim Atkins, "Adventures in Architecture: Il Duomo: Brunelleschi and the Dome of Santa Maria del Fiore," *AIA Architect This Week* 15 (January 25, 2008).

19. Jones, Sereni, and Ricci, "Building Brunelleschi's Dome," 42–43.

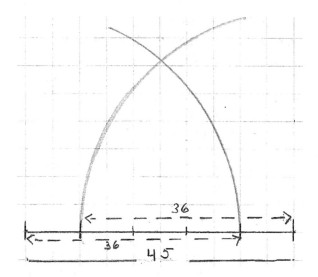

FIGURE 5 *Quinto Arcuto:* The line represents 45 meters divided into five parts. Each arc starts with a compass point at one end of the line and opens up to the fourth of the five parts to create the arc. The compass is then placed on the other end of the line, and the second arc drawn in the same way.

FIGURE 6 The Pantheon, Rome. External view of dome (there are additional images of the Pantheon in the appendix at the end of this document).

research; however, many clues are contained in the Vitruvius reading. That said, here are some things to think about.

1. Standardizing things (molds, measures, and shapes) is very helpful.
2. Paying attention to the properties (weight, strength, density, porosity, etc.) of different materials can make all the difference.
3. Arches and domes were often made using a technique called centering. With this method you built an armature (a lightweight frame) over which the stones or bricks were laid, and once the final piece (the keystone at the top of the arch) was inserted, then the armature was removed. There are many online resources illustrating how this works. You might check them out or look for the YouTube video *MIT Masonry Research—vault decentering.*

4. In addition to the structure used for centering, scaffolds were used to create work platforms.
5. What everyone needs to keep in mind are the types of available materials: local, reusable as you went along, or that could span large areas or be connected in some way to reach across wherever space was necessary to span while remaining stable, and that could support pulleys and similar types of contraptions that would help raise and move various objects and maneuver them into place.

FIGURE 7 Hagia Sophia, Istanbul.

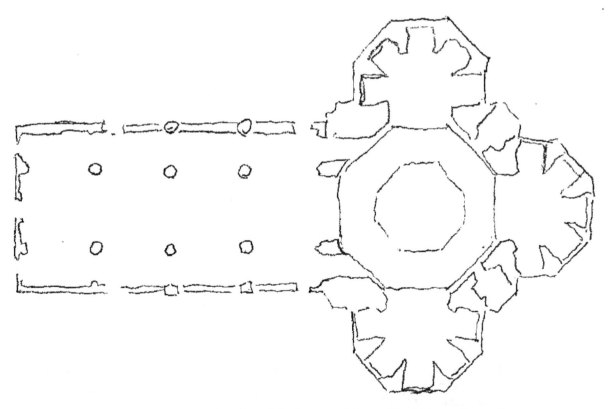

FIGURE 8 Santa Maria del Fiore plan with outline of the hexagonal dome. After Haines 1989, p. 98.

Competition Announcement

19 Agosto 1418

Citizens of Firenze, hear the call for an open competition for the rights to construct the dome of our beloved Cathedrale di Santa Maria del Fiore. The process of completing the church has been ongoing for over 100 years. Fifty years ago we selected the dome design put forth by Neri di Fioravanti, whose model sits in the side aisle of the cathedral. Now the time has come for us to begin the construction of this great work that will bring fame and honor to God and the city of Florence.[20] We request of those who wish to participate that they please provide drawn plans and a model for the vaulting of the Great Dome. Please focus on needs for centering, and address all anticipated needs for armature, scaffolding, or other solution and for any proposed lifting devices necessary for the construction, execution, and completion[21] of the dome by the end of September. The winner will receive 200 florins[22] if their model is used.

20. A common formulation in terms of what the city wanted from this major public undertaking. See Haines, "Brunelleschi and Bureaucracy," 6.

21. After Fanelli and Fanelli, *Brunelleschi's Cupola*, 15.

22. Two hundred florins would be approximately what a skilled craftsperson might earn in two years.

3

The Game

Because this is a short-format game, the focus is concentrated on the interdisciplinary nature of common knowledge at the dawn of the Renaissance. You are asked to consider the many overlapping skills that individuals brought to major ventures, like the construction of the dome and how citizens who were not "experts" whether as architects or engineers might have made decisions regarding the project. The new humanistic bent to studies that give more weight to creativity, ingenuity, and a reverence for the past as well as to the more classic fields of study such as rhetoric and math come together here as you make the case (with models and sketches as well as words) for the best way to approach the challenge of constructing the dome.

Artists will be making the case for the aesthetics of the project as well as considering new ways of representing the world such as the use of linear perspective recently demonstrated to great acclaim by Filippo Brunelleschi and now being used not only in traditional paintings but in the decorative programs of public buildings such as the doors to the baptistry being crafted by Lorenzo Ghiberti. Linear perspective is a very new idea at this time. It uses geometry to help artists create a more realistic and natural sense of depth and space in their works. Until now, depth was often shown by putting things that are meant to be farther away higher up on the image. Now the idea is to imitate what the eye really sees by establishing a point usually in the lower third of the painting that will act as a "vanishing point." That is, as we experience the world, things that are farther away are smaller and less distinct. The vanishing point should serve as that guide to the point at which the things drawn decrease to infinity. This is very challenging to do, but it was now being applied to building sketches as well as paintings and drawings of everything from landscapes to still lives. Does this new technique help in understanding the proposed process for building the dome or in its decoration?

Craftsmen and artisans will be looking to demonstrate how their talents can be put to use in new ways. They might be looking to see how their skills as goldsmiths, sculptors, masons, or weavers might be adapted to make machinery that will help speed along the building process. Will these proposals draw on the foundations of the past while also looking to the future in innovative ways?

Citizens who are interested in "natural philosophy" (as science was referred to) might be considering how the new structure might play into their goals to incorporate the building into their experiments. Is this the proper use of a religious building, or is there no conflict in using such a building to further science?

Merchants and more scholarly intellectual characters will be thinking about the scale of the project and supply chain. Getting materials to the building site and ready to use when needed is a major logistical undertaking. Can it be done in a way that will demonstrate the mercantile acumen for which the city is known? What about how this megaproject will reflect on the honor and prestige of the city? Are you concerned with how the city's investment in this enormous project stands as a statement to the ideals that Florence and Florentines stand for? What if the proposed idea is "too grandiose"? What will failure mean? Is the project too lavish? Is that morally wrong to show off in that way, or is the grandeur of the dome a reflection of all that is right with your city? Does the project build on and reflect the glory of Florence's Roman past or does it overshadow it in some way? These are very disparate areas of endeavor and thought, and yet they brought together personal and civic ambition with the ideals of the day in a unique and lasting way.

Theoretically, each of the teams contending for the commission could come up with the same solution to building the dome. The question is, who can illustrate and explain their plans in the most convincing way? The mock-ups or models provided or the "proof of concept"

offered is what is being judged. The judges must decide who has best explained what they are proposing in the clearest terms and answer questions about their proposal. In weighing the final decision, the citizens of Florence (that is, the jury which includes everyone but the people on the competing teams) must keep in mind the major humanistic principles that they have been espousing (historical foundations, civic pride, and communal work ethic, creativity, and human ingenuity) and select the proposal (or aspects of it) that they think best responds to the city's needs. In handing down the decision, the Opera must caucus first with all the members of the jury on their vote and perhaps try to work through a compromise before making a final announcement regarding what the jury has decided. They must make very clear *why* the jury has selected what or whom they have. In response to that decision, the winning team may elect to accept or reject the final decision based on whether they feel their ideas have been respected or compromised.

RULES AND PROCEDURES

Objectives and Victory Conditions

In order to win, you need to achieve your objective(s). In general this means you must either be on the team with the winning proposal or be in support of that team. The process of deciding who wins requires that the competing teams make good cases for their projects but also that they listen to and incorporate comments from the jury. Suggestions and cooperation among all participants may influence the final decision. Thus it is important to listen to one another and to speak with one another not only in class but perhaps outside of it as well.

Some roles have personal objectives that focus on highlighting particular issues or blocking the discussion of particular issues. As in any community, not all members like each other, and sometimes personal rivalries can change the course of

FIGURE 9 Procession for the Festa di San Giovanni by Giorgio Vasari, located in the Palazzo Vecchio in Florence.

FIGURE 10 Procession, Festa di San Giovanni with *palio* flags by Giovanni Toscani in the Bargello Museum.

events. Any person with personal goals gets a personal victory if they achieve their personal objective(s). There may be some less-than-upright activities which, if brought to light, will cause a character to lose. In addition, there will be a prize for the best *palio*, and all members of the guild that produces it will be rewarded. This means that you can in fact win at some aspects of the game and not at others.

Other Rules

Tommaso Parentucelli will organize, lead, and preside over the procession for the Festa di San Giovanni and the discussion that will take place on the first session of game play (session 3). He will moderate the discussion and select and award the prize for the best *palio*.[1] On sessions 2 and 3 of

1. Together with the GM.

game play (sessions 4–5), the members of the Opera will preside, moderating and leading discussion and questioning of the three teams competing for the commission. In conjunction with the jury (all characters not on one of the three competing teams or on the Opera) they will decide on the winning entry and announce the award.

Figures 9 and 10 provide you with examples of the piazza between the church (with the original façade as seen in the image in chapter 1) and the baptistry. Figure 9 shows Florentines engaged in the procession of San Giovanni itself, and figure 10 shows examples of *palios* in use as part of the same festival. Use these as documents to help you consider what you will do or make for your own procession.

BASIC OUTLINE OF THE GAME

Schedule

Session 1 (setup): Background on Florentine history, politics, and humanism (roles distributed).
Read gamebook background and rules as well as Bruni, Vergerius, and Dati. Start Vitruvius (excerpts) Book 1.
Session 2 (setup): Renaissance Art and Architecture. Faction meetings. Prepare for the Festa di San Giovanni.
Vitruvius; Books 2 and 10.
Session 3 (game play): June 24, 1418: The Festa di San Giovanni. Procession to be followed by a blessing. Parentucelli presents award for best *palio*. This is followed by speeches by all indeterminates who are not members of the Opera. Speeches focus on what each individual wants this project to reveal in terms of the needs of the citizenry and humanistic values to which they subscribe. There will be a full discussion of the ideas presented. If there is time, members of the Opera can remind the teams of the criteria listed in the announcement.

Session 4 (game play): September 1418: Members of the Opera will preside and lay out what they are looking for. Teams in the competition will present their proposals followed by questions and discussion by the whole jury (everyone else). Members of the Opera will summarize what they have seen.
Session 5 (game play and debriefing): The Opera leads discussion with the jury and then votes for the best submission (this last part in private). They then summarize the decision of the whole jury for everyone and announce the winner of the contest and appoint a foreman. [Note that it is possible that a winning team may refuse to accept the commission based on the conditions proposed.] Debriefing.

The schedule is broken down into three parts. First, there are two setup sessions focused on preparing players. These sessions are devoted to understanding the historical context in which the game unfolds and the basics of the new ideas of humanism just being explored at this time. The second of these sessions will explore some of the important ideas in art and architecture developing at this time as well as looking back at some earlier examples. Classes will also learn some basic terms used in discussing architecture (when in doubt, check the glossary in the appendix). For classes that do not focus on art and architecture, this is an especially good time to explore some of the structures that were extant (see images in the appendix for further ideas) and some of the building methods used. For classes that have already covered much of this material as part of their syllabus, this is a good time to explore the writings of early humanist scholars in greater detail. It is possible that your professor may choose to collapse the setup day into a single session or spread it out over a third day. The third through fifth sessions constitute the game itself followed by a debriefing.

SESSION 1: HISTORICAL CONTEXT

Reading for class: Background on Florentine history, politics, and humanism, game rules, and Bruni, Vergerius, and Dati. Start Vitruvius (excerpts) Book 1. Pay particular attention the historical narrative.

In class you will do the following:

Review the historical context in which the game unfolds including the ideas of humanism.

Receive role sheets and roster (some instructors may decide to distribute roles before this preparatory session starts).

SESSION 2: RENAISSANCE ART AND ARCHITECTURE

Reading for class: Vitruvius; Books 2 and 10. Explore images in the appendix and any files provided by your professor.

In class you will do the following:

Explore some of the basic building options available and look at images of structures that would be known to people living at this time. After that you will break into groups for faction meetings. Since people take part in different social groupings, the meetings should be timed such that 10 minutes or so should be given to meeting with the major game factions (competition teams and indeterminates) so that people can become acquainted and the teams competing for the commission can get to work right away researching their options and then developing plans and models. After everyone has a chance to meet and exchange basic information in this first moment, students will regroup for another 10 to 15 minutes or so as guilds to once again exchange basic information and sort out planning for the procession of San Giovanni.

All students except for Tommaso Parentucelli are a member of a guild in addition to being on a competition team or an indeterminate. Indeterminates can be members of the Opera (all the members of the Opera are by definition part of the Arte della Lana, as the Opera is a subgroup of the guild that oversees the construction of the church), or

individual members of the jury. As in life, we all have multiple groups with whom we work or interact. Members of the teams competing for the commission will belong to their team but also to various guilds depending on their expertise and/or background, and all indeterminates belong to a guild based on their profession and/or background. These dual affiliations may mean you need to meet with different groups of people after class (or through other means of communication) if there is not enough time in class to work with all groups.

SESSION 3: FEAST OF SAN GIOVANNI, JUNE 24, 1418 (PIAZZA BETWEEN THE BAPTISTRY AND THE CHURCH)

Before class: All guilds will have completed creating their *palios* and guild flags.

In class: All indeterminates will come prepared to talk about their ideals and desires for the dome utilizing the Bruni, Vergerius, and Dati texts.

The procession for the Festa di San Giovanni will be presided over by Tommaso Parentucelli. He is in charge of organizing the festivities and the procession and helping to guide the discussions regarding what citizens want from this challenging undertaking, and he will award a prize for the best *palio* (the prize should be decided together with the GM). The work of making *palios* and guild banners will take place outside of class, and instructions and plans for the procession can be transmitted by working together outside of class, via email, your class management site, or other social media. Parentucelli should verify plans with his or her professor and then be sure to communicate with classmates so everyone is prepared. Once everyone has processed into the classroom, presentations and discussions begin.

The speakers (all the individual indeterminates—that is, everyone except those people on the teams bidding for the commission or those from the Opera) are charged with discussing why this project is so important for the city and for sharing their ideas and expertise. This is a place to explore in discussion the ideas put forth by Bruni, Vergerius, and Dati. This may entail speaking in more general terms about the importance of this work for the city, how civic responsibilities are important to all citizens in Florence, how creativity and respect for the past might influence what an individual wants from this project. Various individuals may also have personal agendas that with regard to the decorations or machines that might be used or the standardization of work and so on. After each person has spoken, there should be some time devoted to questions and discussion using the texts mentioned above, as they might influence a big project of this nature, as well as forwarding any personal goals your character may have. If this is played in a particularly large class, it may be necessary to cap the time each person has to speak and/or leave all questions and discussions until everyone has spoken.

SESSIONS 4–5: MEETING IN THE OPEN SPACE OF THE TRANSEPT FROM WHICH THE DOME WILL RISE, SEPTEMBER 14, 1418

Before class: All competing teams will have prepared submissions.

In class: Each team will present their project, and each member of those teams will be prepared to help discuss how their project works and perhaps details about the decorative program. They should be prepared to refer to their Vitruvius and, where appropriate, Vergerius and other texts. All indeterminates must be prepared to ask questions of those presenting their projects and use their texts to inform their questions and final decisions.

At the second meeting, time will have moved forward a few months, and we find ourselves in September 1418. The time has come to hear proposals for building the dome. The drum is ready, and so the vaulting needs to start. To solve this problem, the Opera has called for the competition (note that the announcement in the section above includes all the instructions regarding what each submission should include) that you have prepared for.

Who will have the winning design? Who will have the vision and the skills to create and build the dome but also to create the new machinery necessary to raise and place materials so high in the air? That is the challenge for all of the entrants in the competition. Each group will have researched how other domes have been built or come up with their own original ideas or tweaks to existing practice. Each group will present to the jury its proposal. This may include models, examples of equipment, or other demonstrations to help people imagine what they plan to do. Models or portions of models can be made out of cardboard, blocks, clay, wire, wood or any material that can be stacked or otherwise molded to create a model. These can be of the dome but also of equipment that might be used. A three-dimensional model is nice, but not necessary. Sketches or drawings could also be effective, whether of equipment or the dome. Sometimes a small portion of something as proof of concept can work too.

The members of the Opera del Duomo are in charge of the whole project, as they have been for all these many years. They are responsible for managing the proceedings starting on session 2 under the guidance of Battista d'Antonio. The Opera together with the citizens not on the competition teams make up the jury who will decide which plan will win. They will do this in game session 5. Once all the proposals are presented, the jury will confer to decide who will build the dome (that means all the members of the Opera plus all indeterminates) as well as who will be the foreman (this could be more than one person) for this phase of the project. While Battista d'Antonio is currently the foreman for a section of the current cathedral construction, it is not a given that this new commission will automatically fall to him (or anyone else). The winner will be announced by the Opera. The Opera will give a clear explanation for its choice. If the decision is not a straight-out acceptance of one team's plan as is, then those offered the commission will have a chance to accept or decline the job.

Debriefing: After the winner has been announced, the debriefing will start. Everyone will have an opportunity to reveal the motives and strategies they used (or attempted to use) to achieve victory. You may be asked to justify why you voted as you did either in discussion or in writing. In addition, your professor will provide information about how the game adhered to or deviated from historical events. Finally, your professor will clarify what actually happened in history and how things developed following the competition.

ASSIGNMENTS

Everyone participates in the creation of a *palio* (or *palio* and *gonfalone* [guild crest banner]) for their *arte*. The guild banner is your *arte* insignia. A *palio* is the vertical banner created for special occasions, in this case the Festa di San Giovanni. There is an example of such banners in the Toscano image above which you might use for ideas. The *palio* (and guild banner if created) will be carried in the procession on the Festa di San Giovanni, and a winner for best *palio* will be awarded by Tommaso Parentucelli.

Everyone has one individual paper to write and one major presentation of their ideas to make based on their roles and the goals and objectives of their characters. Specific guidance is found within the role sheet. The paper accompanies the presentations, but it does not necessarily have to be identical to that presentation. You may elaborate on certain points (particularly in response to what others have said) when you are giving your presentation. The key, of course, is to convince others to support your position *using the texts provided* and any other outside research you have done to bolster your argument. If the ideas in your paper need to change in response to what is actually happening in the room, then adjust as necessary for the presentation. You are also expected to ask questions and respond to others in the natural course of the discussion, always keeping your character's goals in mind and the information relevant to the topic and the time period. The more you use your texts to support your ideas, the stronger your argument will be. Of course, people may give additional speeches at any moment that moves them.

Your paper allows you to pull together the ideas you are trying to get across using the texts at your disposal and any other research that you do. The more information you have, the stronger your ideas will be and thus the more confident you will be in your presentation. You want to aim to "use" the information, not simply repeat it. Your papers should include a minimum of three direct references to the major texts for this activity, and you should use at least two different texts. Each reference (whether a paraphrase of ideas or a direct quote) should be accompanied by a citation, and there should be a full bibliography of all sources used at the end of your paper (these are basic expectations for your written work, but they are subject to modification by your professor).

All papers should be written in the first person, as the character you embody and in *your* present (i.e., 1418). You may use texts and images available up to that date, but you cannot quote or rely on ideas or information that was not available to someone living in 1418.

It is possible that you will find new terms used in this book and in your texts. If you are not sure of the meaning of something, don't skip it; look it up. Understanding the terms is key to understanding your roles and the ideas that are the heart of this activity. There is a glossary included with this game book, and there are websites with definitions of architectural terms that you may find helpful to use.

4

Roles and Factions

ROLES

Each of you will receive a role. This provides you with key information about who you are and who your allies and enemies may be. As people in any community, everything about you is not obvious to everyone else. Some things about you are private and will be apparent to others only through your actions and interactions. Some activities that you engage in or discussions you have may require you to use some tact and to be circumspect. Most of the roles in the game are based on real people. A few are composites of individuals or invented based on names and professions of real people about which more concrete information is not available and thus use information for people with similar jobs or situations in life.

Your role does not provide 100 percent of the information you need to be successful. In fact, it is simply a foundation or framework. To be successful you will have to do more research on your character (or people like your character). Research is critical to your success. You will need to explore the literature that these early humanists read, look at the "new" books by the "ancients" that have been discovered (perhaps even those mentioned earlier in this game book in addition to the assigned texts), and explore the ideas and techniques that these new fonts of information have put on the table. You may also want to look at paintings or sculpture, as they too are texts that can be read and deciphered for information. Of course you are doing this from the perspective of your character. This is challenging, but challenges can be a lot of fun to master. The more you understand the primary materials and can use the ideas found in them to voice your arguments or create your plans or point to examples of things that support your ideas, the stronger your position will be and the easier you will find it to embody your character.

You may find that people's names seem a little odd. Sometimes people's names include references to familial relationships, locations of birth, family ancestry or to professions. Think of someone whose

TABLE 2 Factions, roles, and affiliations

Name and Faction	Profession	Guild[a]
Team Brunelleschi		
Filippo Brunelleschi (team leader)	goldsmith	Arte della Seta 5
Nanni d'Banco	sculptor	Arte dei Maestri di Pietra 8
Donatello	sculptor	Arte della Seta 5
Pierone Fancello	stonecutter	Arte dei Maestri di Pietra 8
Chiaro d'Andrea	carpenter	Arte dei Legnaioli 9
Team Ghiberti		
Lorenzo Ghiberti (team leader)	goldsmith	Arte della Seta 5
Giovanni d'Prato	humanist	Arte dei Giudici e Notai 1
Bartolomeo dallo Studio	carpenter	Arte dei Legnaioli 9
Salvatore di Piero	mason	Arte dei Maestri di Pietra 8
Domenico di Sandrino	stonecutter	Arte dei Maestri di Pietra 8
Team d'Arrigo		
Giuliano d'Arrigo (team leader)	painter	Arte dei Medici e Speziali 6
Jacopo della Querca	sculptor	Arte dei Medici e Speziali 6
Bertino di Piero	stonecutter	Arte dei Maestri di Pietra 8
Bartolomeo di Francesco	carpenter	Arte dei Legnaioli 9
Francesco di Giovanni	mason	Arte dei Maestri di Pietra 8
L'Opera del Duomo		
Battista d'Antonio	foreman	Arte della Lana 4
Lorenzo d'Prado	lawyer	Arte della Lana 4
Simone di Francesco di Filicaia	notary	Arte della Lana 4
Migliore di Tommaso	treasurer	Arte della Lana 4
Schiatta Ridolfi	laborer	Arte della Lana 4

(continued)

TABLE 2 (*continued*)

Name and Faction	Profession	Guild[a]
Fillipozzo Bastari	scribe	Arte della Lana 4

Indeterminates

Name and Faction	Profession	Guild[a]
Tommaso Parentucelli	humanist	—
Paolo Uccello	painter	Arte dei Medici e Speziali 6
Gherardo di Matteo Doni	laborer	Arte della Seta 5
Leonardo Bruni	humanist	Arte dei Giudici e Notai 1
Niccolo Niccoli	humanist	Arte dei Giudici e Notai 1
Bonaccorso Pitti	merchant	Arte dei Calimala 2
Cosimo de' Medici	banker	Arte del Cambio 3
Pardo da Volterra	kilnsman-brickmaker	Arte dei Maestri di Pietra 8
Lorenzo di Bicci	painter	Arte dei Medici e Speziali 6
Gregorio Dati	merchant	Arte del Calimala 2
Paolo Toscanelli	mathematician	Arte dei Medici e Speziali 6
Alberto Battisti	humanist	Arte dei Giudici e Notai 1
Palla Strozzi	banker	Arte del Cambio 3
Giovanni Medici	banker	Arte del Cambio 3
Bartolo di Marco da Campi	kilnsman-brickmaker	Arte dei Maestri di Pietra 8
Bernardo Ciuffagni	sculptor	Arte dei Maestri di Pietra 8
Michelozzo di Bartolomeo Michelozzi	architect and sculptor	Arte dei Maestri di Pietra 8
Niccolo d'Uzzano	politician	Arte dei Giudici e Notai 1
Rinaldo degli Albizzi	politician	Arte dei Calimala 2

[a] Numbers refer to chart of guilds in table 1.

name might be Sam from North Salem, or David, son of Arthur. You might also find names like Charles the bricklayer. (This is not as strange as you might think. Perhaps you know or have heard of someone with a last name like Smith or Cooper, both of which are professions.) All characters in this game have a first name, a last name, and an indication of what their profession is. Read carefully, and ask your professor if you are confused about names or titles.

There are four factions and a large number of indeterminates in this game.

Three factions are competing to win the contract to build the dome. These groups are headed by Filippo Brunelleschi, Lorenzo Ghiberti, and Giuliano d'Arrigo (called Pesello). The goal for the members of these three teams is to win the right to construct the dome. The Opera del Duomo, led by Battista d'Antonio, is also a faction, because it represents the supervisory members of the Arte della Lana overseeing this project, even though members of the Opera are indeterminates in terms of not having a starting position regarding who should win.

Everyone else, that is, all the illustrious citizens of Florence, humanists, merchants, bankers, and artists, are indeterminates and together with the Opera constitute the jury. They are there to decide who should get the commission. The members of the Opera are overseeing the construction of the cathedral. They have issued the competition announcement and assembled the jury. They manage the competition, as they have called for it, and ultimately, they will be supervising whatever project is approved. All other individual roles are simply members of the jury. If you are an indeterminate, your victory objective may simply be to support the winning proposal, or you may have additional private goals that are outlined on your role sheet. You can find a list of characters and their factions, professions, and guild affiliations in table 2.

FACTIONS

Everyone has multiple alliances in life, and we all experience different social environments and situations in the course of a day (or our lives). Not all citizens in Florence admire one another, and not all of them are happy about having to work together. Some are outright competitive with one another. Some folks are on the straight and narrow, upright citizens that all admire; others, perhaps not so much. Who is who? That will be for you to figure out in the conversations you have with your fellow citizens in the cafés and piazzas and palazzos of town (i.e., outside of class) or other public forums (in class). Just as in life today, no one has all the maps, rules, or understanding. We are all in the process of figuring things out as we go and as we live through different experiences. When in doubt, go back to your texts and research. Nearly all you need to know is there; you just have to use it.

5

Core Texts

The excerpt from Paul Vergerius's work that you have below provides you with one set of guidelines for what a humanist education should include and thus shares with us the ideals that humanists were striving for. You will notice that in many ways these same fields are important in our liberal arts education right down to the present day. It might be worth noting that this was a time before the term "scientist" had been coined and when those who studied math and the natural world were considered natural philosophers. It was the contention of people like Vergerius that these sets of studies were what would make for good citizens because virtue and wisdom were seen as hallmarks of the kind of citizens they were trying to cultivate. Why does Vergerius think that this sort of education had to start early in life, and is it only for the young? Why is history seen as both practical and useful? Which of the liberal arts teaches true freedom? These are just few ideas to consider while reading the excerpts below.

PETRUS PAULUS VERGERIUS, ON NOBLE MANNERS AND LIBERAL STUDIES (CA. 1404)

Excerpts from the Original Electronic Text at the website of the Hanover Historical Texts Project.

Petrus Paulus Vergerius (1370–1444) was a wandering scholar and teacher who traveled widely in Italy and Northern Europe. In the early fifteenth century, he authored the first Renaissance treatise systematically outlining a humanist education program. The treatise, **On Noble Manners and Liberal Studies,** *was actually a letter Vergerius wrote to Ubertinus, son of Francesca Carrara, the lord of Padua, to guide him in his education. In the letter, Vergerius recommends to the young lord virtually all of the disciplines in the medieval liberal arts curriculum—the trivium (grammar, rhetoric, and logic), quadrivium (arithmetic, geometry, astronomy, and music)—and acknowledges his respect for the advanced professional disciplines of medicine, law, and theology. But his emphasis is on rhetoric (or eloquence) and on the ancient disciplines of* *history and moral philosophy, humanities disciplines that were thought to be highly practical. Treatises on education proliferated during the Renaissance, but Vergerius's treatise remained a highly popular one for about 150 years. Today, historians see the humanists educational program, studia humanitatis or the study of humanity, as a defining characteristic of the humanist movement. Humanists believed that the right education can genuinely ennoble individuals and encourage virtue and wisdom, objectives that the arid, abstruse, logic-chopping scholastic program of the Middle Ages failed to achieve. Humanists took widely different positions on philosophical, social, and political issues, but they agreed in their support of the kind of educational program outlined by Vergerius.*

[Note the value of liberal studies here and that they are not simply acquired but applied and necessary.]

[1] We call those studies liberal which are worthy of a free man; those studies by which we attain and practice virtue and wisdom; that education which calls forth, trains and develops those highest gifts of body and of mind which ennoble men, and which are rightly judged to rank next in dignity to virtue only. For to a vulgar temper gain and pleasure are the one aim of existence, to a lofty nature, moral worth and fame. It is, then, of the highest importance that even from infancy this aim, this effort, should constantly be kept alive in growing minds. For I may affirm with fullest conviction that we shall not have attained wisdom in our later years unless in our earliest we have sincerely entered on its search. Nor may we for a moment admit, with the unthinking crowd, that those who give early promise fail in subsequent fulfillment. This may, partly from physical causes, happen in exceptional cases. But there is no doubt that nature has endowed some children with so keen, so ready an intelligence, that without serious effort they attain to a notable power of reasoning and conversing upon grave and lofty subjects, and

by aid of right guidance and sound learning reach in manhood the highest distinction. On the other hand, children of modest powers demand even more attention, that their natural defects may be supplied by art. But all alike must in those early years, "Dum faciles animi iuvenum, dum mobilis aetas,"[1] whilst the mind is supple, be inured to the toil and effort of learning. Not that education, in the broad sense, is exclusively the concern of youth. Did not Cato think it honourable to learn Greek in later life? Did not Socrates, greatest of philosophers, compel his aged fingers to the lute?

[Note the worry that the young are slow to learn and then tensions between learning and the need to work.]

[2] Our youth of today, it is to be feared, is backward to learn; studies are accounted irksome. Boys hardly weaned begin to claim their own way, at a time when every art should be employed to bring them under control and attract them to grave studies. The Master must judge how far he can rely upon emulation, rewards, encouragement; how far he must have recourse to sterner measures. Too much leniency is objectionable; so also is too great severity, for we must avoid all that terrifies a boy. In certain temperaments—those in which a dark complexion denotes a quiet but strong personality—restraint must be cautiously applied. Boys of this type are mostly highly gifted and can bear a gentle hand. Not seldom it happens that a finely tempered nature is thwarted by circumstances, such as poverty at home, which compels a promising youth to forsake learning for trade; though, on the other hand, poverty is less dangerous to lofty instincts than great wealth. Or again, parents encourage their sons to follow a career traditional in their family, which may divert them from liberal studies; and the customary pursuits of the city in which we dwell exercise a decided influence on our choice. . . .

1. "While docile hearts of the young, as long as the age of the movable"—online translation.

[3] In your own case, Ubertinus, you had before you the choice of training in Arms or in Letters. Either holds a place of distinction amongst the pursuits which appeal to men of noble spirit; either leads to fame and honour in the world. It would have been natural that you, the scion of a House ennobled by its prowess in arms, should have been content to accept your father's permission to devote yourself wholly to that discipline. But to your great credit you elected to become proficient in both alike: to add to the career of arms traditional in your family, an equal success in that other great discipline of mind and character, the study of Literature. . . .

[What are the crucial subjects listed here? Why are these subjects listed here and discussed in the sections that follow?]

[4] We come now to the consideration of the various subjects which may rightly be included under the name of "Liberal Studies." Amongst these I accord the first place to History, on grounds both of its attractiveness and of its utility, qualities which appeal equally to the scholar and to the statesman. Next in importance ranks Moral Philosophy, which indeed is, in a peculiar sense, a "Liberal Art," in that its purpose is to teach men the secret of true freedom. History, then, gives us the concrete examples of the precepts inculcated by philosophy. The one shows what men should do, the other what men have said and done in the past, and what practical lessons we may draw therefrom for the present day. I would indicate as the third main branch of study, Eloquence, which indeed holds a place of distinction amongst the refined Arts. By philosophy we learn the essential truth of things, which by eloquence we so exhibit in orderly adornment as to bring conviction to differing minds. And history provides the light of experience—a cumulative wisdom fit to supplement the force of reason and the persuasion of eloquence. For we allow that soundness of judgment, wisdom of speech, integrity of conduct are the marks of a truly liberal temper.

[5] We are told that the Greeks devised for their sons a course of training in four subjects: letters, gymnastic, music and drawing. Now, of these drawing has no place amongst our liberal studies; except in so far as it is identical with writing (which is in reality one side of the art of Drawing), it belongs to the Painter's profession; the Greeks, as an art-loving people, attached to it an exceptional value.

[6] The Art of Letters, however, rests upon a different footing. It is a study adapted to all times and to all circumstances, to the investigation of fresh knowledge or to the re-casting and application of old. Hence the importance of grammar and of the rules of composition must be recognized at the outset, as the foundation on which the whole study of Literature must rest; and closely associated with these rudiments, the art of Disputation or Logical argument. The function of this is to enable us to discern fallacy from truth in discussion. Logic, indeed, as setting forth the true method of learning, is the guide to the acquisition of knowledge in whatever subject. Rhetoric comes next, and is strictly speaking the formal study by which we attain the art of eloquence; which, as we have just stated, takes the third place amongst the studies especially important in public life. It is now, indeed, fallen from its old renown and is well night [*sic*] a lost art. In the Law Court, in the Council, in the popular Assembly, in exposition, in persuasion, in debate, eloquence finds no place nowadays: speed, brevity, homeliness are the only qualities desired. Oratory, in which our forefathers gained so great glory for themselves and for their language, is despised; but our youth, if they would earn the repute of true education, must emulate their ancestors in this accomplishment.

[7] After Eloquence, we place Poetry and the Poetic Art, which though not without value in daily life and as an aid to oratory, have nevertheless their main concern for the leisure side of existence.

[8] As to Music, the Greeks refused the title of "Educated" to anyone who could not sing or play. Socrates set an example to the Athenian youth, by himself learning to play in his old age; urging the pursuit of music not as a sensuous indulgence, but

as an aid to the inner harmony of the soul. In so far as it is taught as a healthy recreation for the moral and spiritual nature, music is a truly liberal art, and, both as regards its theory and practice, should find a place in education.

[9] Arithmetic, which treats of the properties of numbers, Geometry, which treats of the properties of dimensions, lines, surfaces, and solid bodies, are weighty studies because they possess a peculiar element of certainty. The science of the Stars, their motions, magnitudes and distances, lifts us into the clear calm of the upper air. There we may contemplate the fixed stars, or the conjunctions of the planets, and predict the eclipses of the sun and the moon. The knowledge of Nature—animate and inanimate—, the laws and the properties of things in heaven and in earth, their causes, mutations and effects, especially the explanation of their wonders (as they are popularly supposed) by the unravelling of their causes—this is a most delightful, and at the same time most profitable, study for youth. With these may be joined investigations concerning the weights of bodies, and those relative to the subject which mathematicians call "Perspective."

[10] I may here glance for a moment at the three great professional Disciplines: Medicine, Law, Theology. Medicine, which is applied science, has undoubtedly much that makes it attractive to a student. But it cannot be described as a Liberal study. Law, which is based upon moral philosophy, is undoubtedly held in high respect. Regarding Law as a subject of study, such respect is entirely deserved; but Law as practiced becomes a mere trade. Theology, on the other hand, treats of themes removed from our senses, and attainable only by pure intelligence.

[11] The principal "Disciplines" have now been reviewed. It must not be supposed that a liberal education requires acquaintance with them all: for a thorough mastery of even one of them might fairly be the achievement of a lifetime. Most of us, too, must learn to be content with modest capacity as with modest fortune. Perhaps we do wisely to pursue that study which we find most suited to our intelligence and our tastes, though it is true that we cannot rightly understand one subject unless we can perceive its relation to the rest. The choice of studies will depend to some extent upon the character of individual minds. . . .

From Petrus Paulus Vergerius, De ingenues moribus et liberalibus studiis, trans. by W. H. Woodward, Vittorino da Feltre and other Humanist Educators, (Cambridge: Cambridge University Press, 1897), 102–104, 106–109

LEONARDO BRUNI, *PANEGYRIC OF FLORENCE* (CA. 1404)

(You can also find this at the University of York, UK, website under teaching and history as a pdf.)

In this piece, Bruni is using an old and venerated model of writing called a panegyric. A panegyric is a piece written in overflowing praise of something. Bruni turns to his beloved city to extoll its virtues. Here, we have a short excerpt from a longer piece where Bruni is still using the old practices. He looks to both the history of the city and its noble roots (in his opinion) and the way it stands up to encroaching powers. Some things to think about: Given the writings of Vergerius above, why does Bruni, a well-known and respected scholar, start his piece off wondering if he is up to the job? Bruni is torn between the importance of highlighting Florence's beauty over its political power and strength and that of highlighting its magnificent history or customs and institutions. Why does he think its history and customs are so important?

Laudatio Florentinae Urbis or *Panegyric to the City of Florence* (ca. 1403–1404)

Leonardo Bruni (1370–1444) was born in Arezzo and moved to Florence in the early 1390s, where he initially studied law but then took up humanistic studies under the influence of the chancellor, Coluccio Salutati. Bruni produced translations of historical, philosophical, oratorical, and epistolary texts from Greek and Latin but also wrote his own works, drawing upon these classical models. The

Laudatio Florentinae Urbis *was based upon Aelius Aristides's "Panathenaicus," written in the second century A.D., and offered a panegyric (i.e., a speech or piece of writing that praises someone greatly and does not mention anything bad about them) to the city of Florence. Aristides claimed that Athens acted as a bulwark against the despotism of Persia, and so Bruni argued that the republican city of Florence was fighting a battle against the despotism of Milan, controlled by the Visconti family.*

[Bruni starts by questioning his own capacity to achieve his goal. Although a famous and respected scholar and leader, he is not taking his skills for granted.]

Would that God immortal give me eloquence worthy of the city of Florence, about which I am to speak, or at least equal to my zeal and desire on her behalf; for either one degree or the other would, I think, abundantly demonstrate the city's magnificence and splendour. Florence is of such a nature that a more distinguished or more splendid city cannot be found on the entire earth, and I can easily tell about myself, I was never more desirous of doing anything in my life. So I have no doubt at all that if either of these wishes were granted, I should be able to describe with elegance and dignity this very beautiful and excellent city. But because everything we want and the ability granted us to attain what we wish are two different things, we will carry out our intention as well as we can, so that we appear to be lacking in talent rather than in will.

Indeed, this city is of such admirable excellence that no one can match his eloquence with it. But we have seen several good and important men who have spoken concerning God himself, whose glory and magnificence the speech of the most eloquent man cannot capture even in the smallest degree. Nor does this vast superiority keep them from trying to speak insofar as they are able about such an immense magnitude. Therefore, I too shall seem to have done enough if, marshalling all competence, expertise, and skill that I have eventually

acquired after so much study, I devote my all to praising this city, even though I clearly understand that my ability is such that it can in no way be compared with the enormous splendour of Florence. Therefore many orators say that they themselves do not know where to begin.

This now happens to me not only as far as words are concerned but also concerning the subject itself.

For not only are there various things connected one with another, here and there, but also any one of them is so outstanding and in some way so distinguished that they seem to vie for excellence among themselves. Therefore, it is not an easy thing to say which subject is to be treated first. If you consider the beauty or splendour of the city, nothing seems more appropriate to start with than these things. Or if you reflect upon its power and wealth, then you will think these are to be treated first. And if you contemplate its history, either in our own day or in earlier times, nothing can seem so important to begin with as these things. When indeed you consider Florentine customs and institutions, you judge nothing more important than these. These matters cause me concern, and often when I am ready to speak on one point, I recall another and am attracted to it. Hence, they furnish me no opportunity to decide which topic to put first. But I shall seize upon the most apt and logical place to begin the speech, even though I do indeed believe that other topics would not have provided an improper point of departure.

Section 1
Bruni describes the city's beauty at great length.

[This section describes characteristics of Florentine citizens.]

Section 2
Therefore, now that we have described what Florence is, we should next consider what manner of citizens there are here. As one usually does in

discussing an individual, so we want to investigate the origins of the Florentine people and to consider from what ancestor the Florentines derived and what they have accomplished at home and abroad in every age. As Cicero says: "Let's do it this way, let's begin at the beginning."

What, therefore, was the stock of these Florentines? Who were their progenitors? By what mortals was this outstanding city founded? Recognize, men of Florence, recognize your race and your forebears.

Consider that you are, of all races, the most renowned. For other peoples have as forebears refugees or those banished from their fathers' homes, peasants, obscure wanderers, or unknown founders. But your founder is the Roman people—the lord and conqueror of the entire world. Immortal God, you have conferred so many good things on this one city so that everything—no matter where it happens or for what purpose it was ordained—seems to redound to Florence's benefit.

For the fact that the Florentine race arose from the Roman people is of the utmost importance. What nation in the entire world was ever more distinguished, more powerful, more outstanding in every sort of excellence than the Roman people? Their deeds are so illustrious that the greatest feats done by other men seems like child's play when compared to the deeds of the Romans. Their dominion was equal to the entire world, and they governed with the greatest competence for many centuries, so that from a single city comes more examples of virtue than all other nations have been able to produce until now.

In Rome there have been innumerable men so outstanding in every kind of virtue that no other nation on earth has ever been equal to it. Even omitting the names of many fine and outstanding leaders and heads of the Senate, where do you find, except in Rome, the families of the Publicoli, Fabricii, Corruncani, Dentati, Fabii, Decii, Camilli, Pauli, Marcelli, Scipiones, Catones, Gracchi, Torquati, and Cicerones? Indeed, if you are seeking nobility in a founder you will never find any people nobler in the entire world than the Roman people; if you are seeking wealth, none more opulent; if you want grandeur and magnificence, none more outstanding and glorious; if you seek extent of dominion, there was no people on this side of the ocean that had not been subdued and brought under Rome's power by force of arms. Therefore, to you, also, men of Florence, belongs by hereditary right dominion over the entire world and possession of your parental legacy. From this it follows that all wars that are waged by the Florentine people are most just, and this people can never lack justice in its wars since it necessarily wages war for the defense and recovery of its own territory. Indeed, these are the sorts of just wars that are permitted by all laws and legal systems. Now, if the glory, nobility, virtue, grandeur, and magnificence of the parents can also make the sons outstanding, no people in the entire world can be as worthy of dignity as are the Florentines, for they are born from such parents who surpass by a long way all mortals in every sort of glory. Who is there among men who would not readily acknowledge themselves subjected to the Roman people? Indeed, what slave or freedman strives to have the same dignity as the children of his lord or master, or hopes to be chosen instead of them? It is evident that it is no trifling ornament to the city of Florence to have had such an outstanding creator and founder for itself and its people.

But at what point in history did the nation of the Florentines arise from the Romans? Now I believe that in the case of royal successions there is a custom observed by most peoples, namely, that the person who is finally declared to be heir to the king must be born at the time his father possessed the royal dignity. Those offspring who are born either before or after are not considered to be the sons of a king, nor are they permitted to have the right of succession to their father's kingdom. Surely whoever rules when in his best and most flourishing condition also accomplish [sic] his most illustrious and glorious deeds. Indeed, it is evident that, for whatever reasons, prosperous times stimulate men's minds and call forth great spirits, so that at such moments in history great men are able to do only what is important and glorious, and what is accomplished then is always especially outstanding.

Accordingly, this very noble Roman colony was established at the very moment when the dominion of the Roman people flourished greatly and when very powerful kings and warlike nations were being conquered by the skill of Roman aims and by virtue. Carthage, Spain, and Corinth were levelled to the ground; all lands and seas acknowledged the rule of these Romans, and these same Romans suffered no harm from any foreign state. Moreover, the Caesars, the Antonines, the Tiberiuses, the Neros—those plagues and destroyers of the Roman Republic—had not yet deprived the people of their liberty.

Rather, still growing there was that sacred and untrampled freedom that, soon after the founding of the colony of Florence, was to be stolen by those vilest of thieves. For this reason I think something has been true and is true in this city more than in any other; the men of Florence especially enjoy perfect freedom and are the greatest enemies of tyrants. So I believe that from its very founding Florence conceived such a hatred for the destroyers of the Roman state and underminers of the Roman Republic that it has never forgotten to this very day. If any trace of or even the names of those corrupters of Rome have survived to the present, they are hated and scorned in Florence.

GORO DATI, "THE STRUCTURE OF THE FLORENTINE GOVERNMENT" (1409)

Goro Dati kept for many years a personal diary of all the goings on in Florence. One part of that was dedicated to the very complex (some might say convoluted) system of government. In reading this description, pay attention to the many ways the Florentines have divided up power and tried to keep it in check. What mechanisms do you find that seem particularly helpful in controlling power?

Source: Goro Dati, Istoria di Firenze dall'anno MCCCLXXX all'anno MCCCCV, ed. Giuseppe Bianchini (Florence: Manni, 1735), bk. 9, pp. 132–44. Translated by Arielle Saiber in Images of Quattrocento Florence, ed. Stefano Ugo Baldassarri and Arielle Saiber (New Haven: Yale University Press, 2000), 45–49.

ON THE ORGANIZATION OF THE DISTRICTS AND THE GONFALONI, ON THE SIGNORI, PRIORI, AND ALL OTHER OFFICES CONCERNING BOTH THE CITY GOVERNMENT AND THE ADMINISTRATION OF THE FLORENTINE TERRITORY; ON THE RETTORI AND THAT WHICH PERTAINS TO THEIR OFFICE

[General introduction and Dati's views of Florence's place in the world.]

One must certainly believe and give heed to what the Bible says in the words of the Psalmist, "Unless the Lord watches over the city, the watchmen stand guard in vain"[2] no matter what we may say about the just and magnificent government of our city, we must always remember that it is the Lord—by His grace and by the prayers of both the glorious Virgin Mary (whose name is more venerated in Florence than anywhere else in the world) and St. John the Baptist, patron of this city—who governs our state and bestows virtues upon men, as well as the rewards they earn. In order to explain this fact, I shall begin by pointing out that our city possesses active virtue, which pertains to the many occupations that we have already mentioned in the course of our discussion. Like the efforts of Martha,[3] this virtue requires prudence. Florence is also, however, endowed with the virtue of contemplation, which brings us closer to God. Mary achieved this proximity to God on account of its charitable acts, and thereby received God's protection and help. I shall first speak of the active

2. Psalms 127:1.
3. See Luke 10:38–42 regarding the episode of the two sisters Martha and Mary.

life, for clarity and order are fundamental to a better understanding of the whole subject.

[Description of how the city is organized socially and politically. This includes the important roles of the different guilds and their occupations and influences.]

The city is divided into four districts, called *quartieri*; Santo Spirito, Santa Croce, Santa Maria Novella, and San Giovanni. Each district is divided into four *gonfaloni* (sixteen altogether), each with its own symbol (one need not list them). Next come the twenty-one *arti*,[4] whose names I shall list here, for it will help us understand many things I shall soon be discussing. The first guild is the Guild of the Lawyers and Notaries, which has a proconsul ranked about its consuls; it is a powerful guild and can be said to be Christendom's center for the notary profession. The great masters, teachers, and authors who have written on this subject have all been from Florence. The center for lawyers is Bologna that of notaries is Florence.

Next in importance is the Guild of the Cloth Merchants. There are more cloth merchants in our city than in any other, and they export large quantities of goods outside of Florence.[5] The third guild is that of the moneychangers, and one can duly say that all the currency of the world passes through the hands of the Florentines, for they have managers who exchange money in all the important economic centers of the world. Then comes the Guild of the Wool Merchants, the members of which produce wool cloth of unrivaled quality and quantity; they are respectable citizens and experts in their field. The fifth guild is that of the silk workers, which includes those who deal in silk and gold—embroidered cloth; goldsmiths [are also part of this guild]. The products of this guild are

spectacular, especially the cloths. The sixth guild is that of apothecaries, doctors, and shopkeepers; it is a guild which boasts a large number of members. The seventh and last of the "major guilds" is that of the furriers.

Then come the fourteen so-called minor guilds, each one organized according to the specific activity of its members. Only one of the minor guilds combines two occupations; those of the tailors and linen dealers. Each of the other occupations, correspondingly, has its own guild; shoemakers, blacksmiths, grocers, butchers, wine merchants, hotel owners, leather dealers, tanners, armorers, locksmiths, masons, carpenters, and bakers.

[Definitions of *signori*, *priori*, and the *gonfaloniere di giustizia* and their roles and terms of service. Pay attention to the clear rules for the election of people to this post. Note also how all the citizens are woven into this process and how information is passed from one group of leaders to the next. Also pay attention to protocol (who can stand where and so on).]

The term *signori* refers to the *priori* of the guilds and the gonfaloniere di giustizia.[6] There are eight priori, two for each district, and one standard-bearer of justice, elected in turn from one of the four districts. During the year, each district chooses an experienced, worthy citizen from among them for the position of standard-bearer. The standard-bearer is the head of the priori and walks in front of them. Only men forty years of age and older are eligible for this post. The morning on which the standard-bearer of justice assumes his office, he receives the Standard of Justice, a large banner of white cloth with a red cross that he must keep in his temporary residence.[7] When

---

4. The guilds.

5. Often called Arte di Calimala, after the street behind Orsanmichele where its storehouse were situated, it dealt mostly in foreign cloths and wool; these materials were imported from northern Europe in an unfinished state, to be refined and then exported to foreign markets.

6. Standard-bearer of justice.

7. As Dati will soon explain, all the signori, immediately upon their election, were required to leave their homes and move into the Palazzo della Signoria, where they had to remain throughout their term in office.

necessary,[8] he must hold the standard while riding, and everyone must follow him and obey his orders.

There are eight priori, six of whom belong to the major guilds and two to the fourteen minor guilds. Two brothers or two relatives from the father's side may not simultaneously be elected to this office. Once the member of a family has been elected, none of his relatives is eligible for one year. Moreover, whoever has been appointed must wait three years from the end of his term before being re-elected. The first term of office starts on January 1 and lasts for two months; the second term of office, consequently, begins March 1, and this is the schedule followed for the whole year, so that each year the *signoria* changes six times. On the morning the new officials assume their offices, all shops in the city are closed and everyone goes to the piazza to meet the old officials who return to their houses, each one of them accompanied by this family, friends, and relatives. Two days before the end of their appointment, the old priori meet with their successors and bring them up to date on the business they have carried out.

During their two months of office the priori reside in the government palace, where they eat, sleep, and assemble each day to discuss and decide the good of the commune. One of them, in turn, holds the office of *proposto* for three days; all the other priori must obey the orders of the proposto, who walks in front of them next to the standard-bearer. During those three days nothing can be carried out without the proposto's approval, for he is the one entitled to propose actions and ratify the council's decisions.

The signori vote using black and white beans. A friar acts as secretary, collecting the beans in a bag that he receives from the hand of each voter without letting the others see its color. The black bean means "yea," the white one "nay." In order for a proposal to pass, two thirds of the beans must be black.

8. During official ceremonies and processions.

Each member of the signoria is assigned a room in the government palace according to his rank and the district from which he comes; the best room is reserved for the standard-bearer. All the signori have a servant who helps them with whatever they may need in their room, during meals and so forth. There are nine servants altogether—very courteous and well-mannered youths who reside in the palace throughout the year. Each member of the signoria, more-over, has two subordinates whom he sends to act as legates. Altogether, the signoria has a hundred subordinates in its service. They wear green uniforms, and they must carry certain banners of the commune during processions, some of them in front of the signori, some behind. They must escort citizens before the signoria whenever ordered to do so. These one hundred officials are commanded by a foreign captain whose title is *capitano dei fanti*; he is highly esteemed, being the head and the general supervisor of so many men. The minor officials of the signoria are also respected, so much so that when one of them is appointed to escort someone who has been sentenced to exile or is convicted for insolvency, no one—either the *rettori*, the other members of the government, or the private citizens—would ever dare do or say anything against that convict. Upon assuming office, the signori have the authority to decide whether to keep these minor officials or replace them.

No one sits at the table of the signoria except the signori themselves and their secretary. Guests, foreign authorities, or ambassadors of foreign lords and communes are [however] sometimes invited to dine at the table. On special occasions, such as religious feasts or the welcoming of important guests, the rettori and certain city officials are allowed to have lunch with the signoria, whose table is said to be well appointed, elegantly served, and orderly, as befits the highest authorities of a government. Each month three hundred florins are spent on the signori's meals. They also enjoy the company of the commune's fifers, musicians, jesters, jugglers, and all sorts of entertainers, though they can rarely indulge in such activities, being continually summoned by the proposto to discuss the needs of the state. They never lack for things to do.

[Pay attention here to the details of the bureaucracy and note where education and learning come in.]

They have a secretary in their service who stays in the palace for two months and sits at their table; his only task is to record the signoria's deliberations. There is also another secretary, however, who by contrast, is elected for life. His aid is requested only when needed, and he is appointed to write down and learn all the laws issued by the signori and the councils of the *collegi*. They have a chancellor who lives in the palace and whose job it is to write all the letters and official documents that the commune sends to princes and governments all over the world. This office is always held by men of great erudition who are also expert in poetry. Both the secretaries and the chancellor need numerous subordinates to see their orders.

[Powers of those in government.]

The signori have unlimited power and authority. While holding office they can do whatever they see fit in emergency situations; normally they simply enforce the commune's laws. Once their term of office is over, they cannot be charged with anything they have done while in service, except for embezzlement or simony. A special official who must come from outside Florence, the *esecutore degli ordini*, is entrusted with the task of verifying any such accusation. If there is not an esecutore in service at the time, it becomes the duty of the podestà.

[Note how these terms of service are different from those listed above and again how citizens play an important role in the execution of the civic duties.]

The sixteen gonfalonieri have a term of office that starts on January 8 and lasts four months. There are three elections a year to the position. The Confalonieri must appear before the signori whenever requested, which basically means every day, and give their advice, just as the cardinals do with the pope. On the morning they assume their office, all the city shops are closed and the signori stand with the rettori by the *ringhiera*[9] outside the palace. Then one of the rettori steps up to another ringhiera, or rather pulpit, and delivers a beautiful oration in honor of the said signoria and the gonfalonieri. Each gonfalonieri is given his own standard, and to the sound of trumpets and fifes they return to their homes, congratulated by the crowd. All citizens follow the gonfalonieri of their own district, whose standard he carries. He is accompanied by three men carrying smaller district banners that have been handed over to them in the course of the ceremony; all they have to do is follow the gonfaloniere whenever necessary. . . .

VITRUVIUS, *THE TEN BOOKS ON ARCHITECTURE* (63 B.C.E.–14 A.D.)

The discovery of this work by Vitruvius was momentous. For years people had wondered how the "ancients" had managed to build the magnificent temples and buildings to be found throughout the Greek and Roman worlds. This book was seen by many as the key, the handbook that would help them understand how those buildings were constructed. Interestingly, this work is not just about construction but also about the quality of materials, about aesthetics of building (choosing the right spot as well as harmony in the structure). You'll note right at the start that Vitruvius calls on the builder to be versed in multiple disciplines, something that would resonate with the new views being developed. In this version there has been some condensing of chapters or skipping of chapters for ease of use. Pay special attention to the different materials and their properties, and machinery and its uses, as that might help you in developing your proposals or in questioning the proposals of others.

9. A tribune with an iron bar where the officials appeared to speak to the crowd.

Marcus Vitruvius Pollio, known simply as Vitruvius, lived from c. 90 to c. 20 B.C.E. He was a military engineer, and his work The Ten Books on Architecture *represents his basic summary of the knowledge and rules regarding the construction of different types of buildings and about the qualities of different building materials. It is his manifesto of sorts, bringing together his expertise in engineering and architecture, his admiration for the work of those in the ancient Greek world that he saw on his travels, and his ideas on what makes the aesthetics of architecture important for citizens of any community. The exact date of original publication is not clear (but within his lifetime), and the work eventually disappeared from circulation at some point to be "rediscovered" in 1414 in a monastery in St. Galen, Switzerland.*

VITRUVIUS
THE TEN BOOKS ON ARCHITECTURE
TRANSLATED BY
MORRIS HICKY MORGAN, PH.D., LL.D.
LATE PROFESSOR OF CLASSICAL PHILOLOGY
IN HARVARD UNIVERSITY
WITH ILLUSTRATIONS AND ORIGINAL DESIGNS
PREPARED UNDER THE DIRECTION OF
HERBERT LANGFORD WARREN, A.M.
NELSON ROBINSON JR. PROFESSOR OF
ARCHITECTURE
IN HARVARD UNIVERSITY
CAMBRIDGE
HARVARD UNIVERSITY PRESS
LONDON: HUMPHREY MILFORD
OXFORD UNIVERSITY PRESS
1914
COPYRIGHT, HARVARD UNIVERSITY PRESS

Excerpts:

[In this section of Book 1, Vitruvius lays out all the many interconnected skills that he feels are required to be a good architect. Note that in his view the requirements are very broad and simply technical skill is not sufficient. Everything from astronomy to music is important to the education of an architect.]

Book 1
Chapter 1
The Education of the Architect

1. The architect should be equipped with knowledge of many branches of study and varied kinds of learning, for it is by his judgment that all work done by the other arts is put to test. This knowledge is the child of practice and theory. Practice is the continuous and regular exercise of employment where manual work is done with any necessary material according to the design of a drawing. Theory, on the other hand, is the ability to demonstrate and explain the productions of dexterity on the principles of proportion.

2. It follows, therefore, that architects who have aimed at acquiring manual skill without scholarship have never been able to reach a position of authority to correspond to their pains, while those who relied only upon theories and scholarship were obviously hunting the shadow, not the substance. But those who have a thorough knowledge of both, like men armed at all points, have the sooner attained their object and carried authority with them.

3. In all matters, but particularly in architecture, there are these two points:—the thing signified, and that which gives it its significance. That which is signified is the subject of which we may be speaking; and that which gives significance is a demonstration on scientific principles. It appears, then, that one who professes himself an architect should be well versed in both directions. He ought, therefore, to be both naturally gifted and amenable to instruction. Neither natural ability without instruction nor instruction without natural ability can make the perfect artist. Let him be educated, skillful with the pencil, instructed in geometry, know much history, have followed the philosophers with attention, understand music, have some knowledge of medicine know the opinions of the jurists, and be acquainted with astronomy and the theory of the heavens.

4. The reasons for all this are as follows. An architect ought to be an educated man so as to leave a more lasting remembrance in his treatises. Secondly, he must have a knowledge of drawing so that he can readily make sketches to show the appearance of the work which he proposes. Geometry, also, is of much assistance in architecture, and in particular it teaches us the use of the rule and compasses, by which especially we acquire readiness in making plans for buildings in their grounds, and rightly apply the square, the level, and the plummet. By means of optics, again, the light in buildings can be drawn from fixed quarters of the sky. It is true that it is by arithmetic that the total cost of buildings is calculated and measurements are computed, but difficult questions involving symmetry are solved by means of geometrical theories and methods.

[*Caryatides* are columns in the shape of women; *Mutules* are flat, horizontally placed blocks—sometimes decorated—that lie below the *Corona*, which is a part of the cornice or the upper part of the building that sits upon and projects out from the columns.]

5. A wide knowledge of history is requisite because, among the ornamental parts of an architect's design for a work, there are many the underlying idea of whose employment he should be able to explain to the inquirers. For instance, suppose him to set up the marble statues of women in long robes, called Caryatides, to take the place of columns, with the mutules and coronas placed directly above their heads, he will give the following explanation to his questioners. Caryae, a state in Peloponnesus, sided with the Persian enemies against Greece; later the Greeks, having gloriously won their freedom by victory in the war, made common cause and declared war against the people of Caryae. They took the town, killed the men, abandoned the State to desolation, and carried off their wives into slavery, without permitting them, however, to lay aside the long robes and other marks of their rank as married women, so that they might be obliged not only to march in the triumph but to appear forever after as a type of slavery, burdened with the weight of their shame and so making atonement for their State. Hence, the architects of the time designed for public buildings statues of these women, placed so as to carry a load, in order that the sin and the punishment of the people of Caryae might be known and handed down even to posterity.

[handwritten margin note: must know history for good, timely art]

6. Likewise the Lacedaemonians under the leadership of Pausanias, son of Agesipolis, after conquering the Persian armies, infinite in number, with a small force at the battle of Plataea, celebrated a glorious triumph with the spoils and booty, and with the money obtained from the sale thereof built the Persian Porch, to be a monument to the renown and valor of the people and a trophy of victory for posterity. And there they set effigies of the prisoners arrayed in barbarian costume and holding up the roof, their pride punished by this deserved affront, that enemies might tremble for fear of the effects of their courage, and that their own people, looking upon this example of their valor and encouraged by the glory of it, might be ready to defend their independence. So from that time on, many have put up statues of Persians supporting entablatures and their ornaments, and thus from that motive have greatly enriched the diversity of their works. There are other stories of the same kind which architects ought to know.

7. As for philosophy, it makes an architect high-minded and not self-assuming, but rather renders him courteous, just, and honest without avariciousness. This is very important, for no work can be rightly done without honesty and incorruptibility. Let him not be grasping nor have his mind preoccupied with the idea of receiving perquisites, but let him with dignity keep up his position by cherishing a good reputation. These are among the precepts of philosophy. Furthermore philosophy treats of physics (in Greek φυσιολογία) where a more careful knowledge is required because the problems which come under this head are numerous and of very different kinds; as, for example, in the case of the conducting of water. For

at points of intake and at curves, and at places where it is raised to a level, currents of air naturally form in one way or another; and nobody who has not learned the fundamental principles of physics from philosophy will be able to provide against the damage which they do. So the reader of Ctesibius or Archimedes and the other writers of treatises of the same class will not be able to appreciate them unless he has been trained in these subjects by the philosophers.

8. Music, also, the architect ought to understand so that he may have knowledge of the canonical and mathematical theory, and besides be able to tune ballistae, catapultae, and scorpiones to the proper key. For to the right and left in the beams are the holes in the frames through which the strings of twisted sinew are stretched by means of windlasses and bars, and these strings must not be clamped and made fast until they give the same correct note to the ear of the skilled workman. For the arms thrust through those stretched strings must, on being let go, strike their blow together at the same moment; but if they are not in unison, they will prevent the course of projectiles from being straight.

9. In theatres, likewise, there are the bronze vessels (in Greek ἠχεῖα) which are placed in niches under the seats in accordance with the musical intervals on mathematical principles. These vessels are arranged with a view to musical concords or harmony, and apportioned in the compass of the fourth, the fifth, and the octave, and so on up to the double octave, in such a way that when the voice of an actor falls in unison with any of them its power is increased, and it reaches the ears of the audience with greater clearness and sweetness. Water organs, too, and the other instruments which resemble them cannot be made by one who is without the principles of music.

10. The architect should also have a knowledge of the study of medicine on account of the questions of climates (in Greek κλίματα), air, the healthiness and unhealthiness of sites, and the use of different waters. For without these considerations, the healthiness of a dwelling cannot be assured. And as for principles of law, he should know those which are necessary in the case of buildings having party walls, with regard to water dripping from the eaves, and also the laws about drains, windows, and water supply. And other things of this sort should be known to architects, so that, before they begin upon buildings, they may be careful not to leave disputed points for the householders to settle after the works are finished, and so that in drawing up contracts the interests of both employer and contractor may be wisely safe-guarded. For if a contract is skillfully drawn, each may obtain a release from the other without disadvantage. From astronomy we find the east, west, south, and north, as well as the theory of the heavens, the equinox, solstice, and courses of the stars. If one has no knowledge of these matters, he will not be able to have any comprehension of the theory of sundials.

11. Consequently, since this study is so vast in extent, embellished and enriched as it is with many different kinds of learning, I think that men have no right to profess themselves architects hastily, without having climbed from boyhood the steps of these studies and thus, nursed by the knowledge of many arts and sciences, having reached the heights of the holy ground of architecture.

12. But perhaps to the inexperienced it will seem a marvel that human nature can comprehend such a great number of studies and keep them in the memory. Still, the observation that all studies have a common bond of union and intercourse with one another, will lead to the belief that this can easily be realized. For a liberal education forms, as it were, a single body made up of these members. Those, therefore, who from tender years receive instruction in the various forms of learning, recognize the same stamp on all the arts, and an intercourse between all studies, and so they more readily comprehend them all. This is what led one of the ancient architects, Pytheos, the celebrated builder of the temple of Minerva at Priene, to say in

his Commentaries that an architect ought to be able to accomplish much more in all the arts and sciences than the men who, by their own particular kinds of work and the practice of it, have brought each a single subject to the highest perfection. But this is in point of fact not realized.

13. For an architect ought not to be and cannot be such a philologian as was Aristarchus, although not illiterate; nor a musician like Aristoxenus, though not absolutely ignorant of music; nor a painter like Apelles, though not unskillful in drawing; nor a sculptor such as was Myron or Polyclitus, though not unacquainted with the plastic art; nor again a physician like Hippocrates, though not ignorant of medicine; nor in the other sciences need he excel in each, though he should not be unskillful in them. For, in the midst of all this great variety of subjects, an individual cannot attain to perfection in each, because it is scarcely in his power to take in and comprehend the general theories of them.

14. Still, it is not architects alone that cannot in all matters reach perfection, but even men who individually practise specialties in the arts do not all attain to the highest point of merit. Therefore, if among artists working each in a single field not all, but only a few in an entire generation acquire fame, and that with difficulty, how can an architect, who has to be skillful in many arts, accomplish not merely the feat—in itself a great marvel—of being deficient in none of them, but also that of surpassing all those artists who have devoted themselves with unremitting industry to single fields?

15. It appears, then, that Pytheos made a mistake by not observing that the arts are each composed of two things, the actual work and the theory of it. One of these, the doing of the work, is proper to men trained in the individual subject, while the other, the theory, is common to all scholars: for example, to physicians and musicians the rhythmical beat of the pulse and its metrical movement. But if there is a wound to be healed or a sick man to be saved from danger, the musician will not call, for the business will be appropriate to the physician. So in the case of a musical instrument, not the physician but the musician will be the man to tune it so that the ears may find their due pleasure in its strains.

16. Astronomers likewise have a common ground for discussion with musicians in the harmony of the stars and musical concords in tetrads and triads of the fourth and the fifth, and with geometricians in the subject of vision (in Greek λόγος ὀπτικός); and in all other sciences many points, perhaps all, are common so far as the discussion of them is concerned. But the actual undertaking of works which are brought to perfection by the hand and its manipulation is the function of those who have been specially trained to deal with a single art. It appears, therefore, that he has done enough and to spare who in each subject possesses a fairly good knowledge of those parts, with their principles, which are indispensable for architecture, so that if he is required to pass judgement and to express approval in the case of those things or arts, he may not be found wanting. As for men upon whom nature has bestowed so much ingenuity, acuteness, and memory that they are able to have a thorough knowledge of geometry, astronomy, music, and the other arts, they go beyond the functions of architects and become pure mathematicians. Hence they can readily take up positions against those arts because many are the artistic weapons with which they are armed. Such men, however, are rarely found, but there have been such at times; for example, Aristarchus of Samos, Philolaus and Archytas of Tarentum, Apollonius of Perga, Eratosthenes of Cyrene, and among Syracusans Archimedes and Scopinas, who through mathematics and natural philosophy discovered, expounded, and left to posterity many things in connection with mechanics and with sundials.

17. Since, therefore, the possession of such talents due to natural capacity is not vouchsafed at random to entire nations, but only to a few great

men; since, moreover, the function of the architect requires a training in all the departments of learning; and finally, since reason, on account of the wide extent of the subject, concedes that he may possess not the highest but not even necessarily a moderate knowledge of the subjects of study, I request, Caesar, both of you and of those who may read the said books, that if anything is set forth with too little regard for grammatical rule, it may be pardoned. For it is not as a very great philosopher, nor as an eloquent rhetorician, nor as a grammarian trained in the highest principles of his art, that I have striven to write this work, but as an architect who has had only a dip into those studies. Still, as regards the efficacy of the art and the theories of it, I promise and expect that in these volumes I shall undoubtedly show myself of very considerable importance not only to builders but also to all scholars.

Chapter 2

[Here we are given an explanation and definition of the concepts that define good architecture. Note that it is the relationship between elements that is important, as is the creator's ability to consider and reflect upon those relationships (reflective thinking and writing are critical to the success of many fields of endeavor, even today).]

The Fundamental Principles of Architecture

1. Architecture depends on Order (in Greek τάξις), Arrangement (in Greek διάθεσις), Eurythmy, Symmetry, Propriety, and Economy (in Greek οἰκονομία).

2. Order gives due measure to the members of a work considered separately, and symmetrical agreement to the proportions of the whole. It is an adjustment according to quantity (in Greek ποσότης). By this I mean the selection of modules from the members of the work itself and, starting from these individual parts of members, constructing the whole work to correspond. Arrangement includes the putting of things in their proper places and the elegance of effect which is due to adjustments appropriate to the character of the work. Its

forms of expression (Greek ἰδέαι) are these: ground plan, elevation, and perspective. A ground plan is made by the proper successive use of compasses and rule, through which we get outlines for the plane surfaces of buildings. An elevation is a picture of the front of a building, set upright and properly drawn in the proportions of the contemplated work. Perspective is the method of sketching a front with the sides withdrawing into the background, the lines all meeting in the center of a circle. All three come of reflection and invention. Reflection is careful and laborious thought, and watchful attention directed to the agreeable effect of one's plan. Invention, on the other hand, is the solving of intricate problems and the discovery of new principles by means of brilliancy and versatility. These are the departments belonging under Arrangement.

3. Eurythmy is beauty and fitness in the adjustments of the members. This is found when the members of a work are of a height suited to their breadth, of a breadth suited to their length, and, in a word, when they all correspond symmetrically.

4. Symmetry is a proper agreement between the members of the work itself, and relation between the different parts and the whole general scheme, in accordance with a certain part selected as standard. Thus in the human body there is a kind of symmetrical harmony between forearm, foot, palm, finger, and other small parts; and so it is with perfect buildings. In the case of temples, symmetry may be calculated from the thickness of a column, from a triglyph, or even from a module; in the ballista, from the hole or from what the Greeks call the περίτρητος; in a ship, from the space between the tholepins διάπηγμά; and in other things, from various members.

5. Propriety is that perfection of style which comes when a work is authoritatively constructed on approved principles. It arises from prescription (Greek: θεματισμῶ), from usage, or from nature. From prescription, in the case of hypaethral edifices, open to the sky, in honor of Jupiter Lightning, the Heaven, the Sun, or the Moon: for these

are gods whose semblances and manifestations we behold before our very eyes in the sky when it is cloudless and bright. The temples of Minerva, Mars, and Hercules, will be Doric, since the virile strength of these gods makes daintiness entirely inappropriate to their houses. In temples to Venus, Flora, Proserpine, Spring-Water, and the Nymphs, the Corinthian order will be found to have peculiar significance, because these are delicate divinities and so its rather slender outlines, its flowers, leaves, and ornamental volutes will lend propriety where it is due. The construction of temples of the Ionic order to Juno, Diana, Father Bacchus, and the other gods of that kind, will be in keeping with the middle position which they hold; for the building of such will be an appropriate combination of the severity of the Doric and the delicacy of the Corinthian.

6. Propriety arises from usage when buildings having magnificent interiors are provided with elegant entrance-courts to correspond; for there will be no propriety in the spectacle of an elegant interior approached by a low, mean entrance. Or, if dentils be carved in the cornice of the Doric entablature or triglyphs represented in the Ionic entablature over the cushion-shaped capitals of the columns, the effect will be spoilt by the transfer of the peculiarities of the one order of building to the other, the usage in each class having been fixed long ago.

7. Finally, propriety will be due to natural causes if, for example, in the case of all sacred precincts we select very healthy neighborhoods with suitable springs of water in the places where the fanes are to be built, particularly in the case of those to Aesculapius and to Health, gods by whose healing powers great numbers of the sick are apparently cured. For when their diseased bodies are transferred from an unhealthy to a healthy spot, and treated with waters from health-giving springs, they will the more speedily grow well. The result will be that the divinity will stand in higher esteem and find his dignity increased, all owing to the nature of his site. There will also be natural propriety in using an eastern light for bedrooms and libraries, a western light in winter for baths and winter apartments, and a northern light for picture galleries and other places in which a steady light is needed; for that quarter of the sky grows neither light nor dark with the course of the sun, but remains steady and unshifting all day long.

8. Economy denotes the proper management of materials and of site, as well as a thrifty balancing of cost and common sense in the construction of works. This will be observed if, in the first place, the architect does not demand things which cannot be found or made ready without great expense. For example: it is not everywhere that there is plenty of pitsand, rubble, fir, clear fir, and marble, since they are produced in different places and to assemble them is difficult and costly. Where there is no pitsand, we must use the kinds washed up by rivers or by the sea; the lack of fir and clear fir may be evaded by using cypress, poplar, elm, or pine; and other problems we must solve in similar ways.

9. A second stage in Economy is reached when we have to plan the different kinds of dwellings suitable for ordinary householders, for great wealth, or for the high position of the statesman. A house in town obviously calls for one form of construction; that into which stream the products of country estates requires another; this will not be the same in the case of money-lenders and still different for the opulent and luxurious; for the powers under whose deliberations the common-wealth is guided dwellings are to be provided according to their special needs: and, in a word, the proper form of economy must be observed in building houses for each and every class.

Chapter 3
The Departments of Architecture

1. There are three departments of architecture: the art of building, the making of timepieces, and the construction of machinery. Building is, in its turn, divided into two parts, of which the first is the

construction of fortified towns and of works for general use in public places, and the second is the putting up of structures for private individuals. There are three classes of public buildings: the first for defensive, the second for religious, and the third for utilitarian purposes. Under defense comes the planning of walls, towers, and gates, permanent devices for resistance against hostile attacks; under religion, the erection of fanes and temples to the immortal gods; under utility, the provision of meeting places for public use, such as harbors, markets, colonnades, baths, theatres, promenades, and all other similar arrangements in public places.

2. All these must be built with due reference to durability, convenience, and beauty. Durability will be assured when foundations are carried down to the solid ground and materials wisely and liberally selected; convenience, when the arrangement of the apartments is faultless and presents no hindrance to use, and when each class of building is assigned to its suitable and appropriate exposure; and beauty, when the appearance of the work is pleasing and in good taste, and when its members are in due proportion according to correct principles of symmetry.

Book 2

[Of the three areas of architecture included here, the art of building and the construction of machinery are the ones that concern us most here. Beyond that, work in brick, pozzolana (a type of mortar), stone, and timber will be of importance to the project of the dome.]

Introduction

5. In my first book, I have said what I had to say about the functions of architecture and the scope of the art, as well as about fortified towns and the apportionment of building sites within the fortifications. Although it would next be in order to explain the proper proportions and symmetry of temples and public buildings, as well as of private houses, I thought best to postpone this until after I had treated the practical merits of the materials out

of which, when they are brought together, buildings are constructed with due regard to the proper kind of material for each part, and until I had shown of what natural elements those materials are composed. But before beginning to explain their natural properties, I will prefix the motives which originally gave rise to buildings and the development of inventions in this field, following in the steps of early nature and of those writers who have devoted treatises to the origins of civilization and the investigation of inventions. My exposition will, therefore, follow the instruction which I have received from them.

Chapter 3
Brick

1. Beginning with bricks, I shall state of what kind of clay they ought to be made. They should not be made of sandy or pebbly clay, or of fine gravel, because when made of these kinds they are in the first place heavy; and, secondly, when washed by the rain as they stand in walls, they go to pieces and break up, and the straw in them does not hold together on account of the roughness of the material. They should rather be made of white and chalky or of red clay, or even of a coarse grained gravelly clay. These materials are smooth and therefore durable; they are not heavy to work with, and are readily laid.

[Good guidance in terms of timing when things can be made and delivered for the challenge of building the dome.]

2. Bricks should be made in Spring or Autumn, so that they may dry uniformly. Those made in Summer are defective, because the fierce heat of the sun bakes their surface and makes the brick seem dry while inside it is not dry. And so the shrinking, which follows as they dry, causes cracks in the parts which were dried before, and these cracks make the bricks weak. Bricks will be most serviceable if made two years before using; for they cannot dry thoroughly in less time. When fresh undried bricks are used in a wall, the stucco covering stiffens and hardens into a permanent

mass, but the bricks settle and cannot keep the same height as the stucco; the motion caused by their shrinking prevents them from adhering to it, and they are separated from their union with it. Hence the stucco, no longer joined to the core of the wall, cannot stand by itself because it is so thin; it breaks off, and the walls themselves may perhaps be ruined by their settling. This is so true that at Utica in constructing walls they use brick only if it is dry and made five years previously, and approved as such by the authority of a magistrate.

[Note that you can make bricks in different shapes and sizes according to need or use.]

3. There are three kinds of bricks. First, the kind called in Greek Lydian, being that which our people use, a foot and a half long and one foot wide. The other two kinds are used by the Greeks in their buildings. Of these, one is called πεντάδωρον, the other τετράδωρον. Δῶρον is the Greek for "palm," for in Greek δῶρον means the giving of gifts, and the gift is always presented in the palm of the hand. A brick five palms square is called "pentadoron"; one four palms square "tetradoron." Public buildings are constructed of πεντάδωρα, private of τετράδωρα.

4. With these bricks there are also half-bricks. When these are used in a wall, a course of bricks is laid on one face and a course of half-bricks on the other, and they are bedded to the line on each face. The walls are bonded by alternate courses of the two different kinds, and as the bricks are always laid so as to break joints, this lends strength and a not unattractive appearance to both sides of such walls.

In the states of Maxilua and Callet, in Further Spain, as well as in Pitane in Asia Minor, there are bricks which, when finished and dried, will float on being thrown into water. The reason why they can float seems to be that the clay of which they are made is like pumice-stone. So it is light, and also it does not, after being hardened by exposure to the air, take up or absorb liquid. So these bricks, being of this light and porous quality, and admitting no moisture into their texture, must by the laws of

nature float in water, like pumice, no matter what their weight may be. They have therefore great advantages; for they are not heavy to use in building and, once made, they are not spoiled by bad weather.

Chapter 4
Sand

1. In walls of masonry the first question must be with regard to the sand, in order that it may be fit to mix into mortar and have no dirt in it. The kinds of pitsand are these: black, gray, red, and carbuncular. Of these the best will be found to be that which crackles when rubbed in the hand, while that which has much dirt in it will not be sharp enough. Again: throw some sand upon a white garment and then shake it out; if the garment is not soiled and no dirt adheres to it, the sand is suitable.

2. But if there are no sandpits from which it can be dug, then we must sift it out from river beds or from gravel or even from the sea beach. This kind, however, has these defects when used in masonry: it dries slowly; the wall cannot be built up without interruption but from time to time there must be pauses in the work; and such a wall cannot carry vaultings. Furthermore, when sea-sand is used in walls and these are coated with stucco, a salty efflorescence is given out which spoils the surface.

3. But pitsand used in masonry dries quickly, the stucco coating is permanent, and the walls can support vaultings. I am speaking of sand fresh from the sandpits. For if it lies unused too long after being taken out, it is disintegrated by exposure to sun, moon, or hoar frost, and becomes earthy. So when mixed in masonry, it has no binding power on the rubble, which consequently settles and down comes the load which the walls can no longer support. Fresh pitsand, however, in spite of all its excellence in concrete structures, is not equally useful in stucco, the richness of which, when the lime and straw are mixed with such sand, will cause it to crack as it dries on account of the great strength of the mixture. But river sand, though useless in "signinum" on account of its

thinness, becomes perfectly solid in stucco when thoroughly worked by means of polishing instruments.

Chapter 5
Lime

1. Sand and its sources having been thus treated, next with regard to lime we must be careful that it is burned from a stone which, whether soft or hard, is in any case white. Lime made of close-grained stone of the harder sort will be good in structural parts; lime of porous stone, in stucco. After slaking it, mix your mortar, if using pitsand, in the proportions of three parts of sand to one of lime; if using river or sea-sand, mix two parts of sand with one of lime. These will be the right proportions for the composition of the mixture. Further, in using river or sea-sand, the addition of a third part composed of burnt brick, pounded up and sifted, will make your mortar of a better composition to use.

2. The reason why lime makes a solid structure on being combined with water and sand seems to be this: that rocks, like all other bodies, are composed of the four elements. Those which contain a larger proportion of air, are soft; of water, are tough from the moisture; of earth, hard; and of fire, more brittle. Therefore, if limestone, without being burned, is merely pounded up small and then mixed with sand and so put into the work, the mass does not solidify nor can it hold together. But if the stone is first thrown into the kiln, it loses its former property of solidity by exposure to the great heat of the fire, and so with its strength burnt out and exhausted it is left with its pores open and empty. Hence, the moisture and air in the body of the stone being burned out and set free, and only a residuum of heat being left lying in it, if the stone is then immersed in water, the moisture, before the water can feel the influence of the fire, makes its way into the open pores; then the stone begins to get hot, and finally, after it cools off, the heat is rejected from the body of the lime.

3. Consequently, limestone when taken out of the kiln cannot be as heavy as when it was thrown in, but on being weighed, though its bulk remains the same as before, it is found to have lost about a third of its weight owing to the boiling out of the water. Therefore, its pores being thus opened and its texture rendered loose, it readily mixes with sand, and hence the two materials cohere as they dry, unite with the rubble, and make a solid structure.

Chapter 6
Pozzolana
[Used as mortar, even today.]

1. There is also a kind of powder which from natural causes produces astonishing results. It is found in the neighborhood of Baiae and in the country belonging to the towns round about Mt. Vesuvius. This substance, when mixed with lime and rubble, not only lends strength to buildings of other kinds, but even when piers of it are constructed in the sea, they set hard under water. The reason for this seems to be that the soil on the slopes of the mountains in these neighbourhoods is hot and full of hot springs. This would not be so unless the mountains had beneath them huge fires of burning sulphur or alum or asphalt. So the fire and the heat of the flames, coming up hot from far within through the fissures, make the soil there light, and the tufa found there is spongy and free from moisture. Hence, when the three substances, all formed on a similar principle by the force of fire, are mixed together, the water suddenly taken in makes them cohere, and the moisture quickly hardens them so that they set into a mass which neither the waves nor the force of the water can dissolve.

2. That there is burning heat in these regions may be proved by the further fact that in the mountains near Baiae, which belongs to the Cumaeans, there are places excavated to serve as sweating-baths, where the intense heat that comes from far below bores its way through the earth, owing to the force of the fire, and passing up appears in these regions, thus making remarkably good sweating-baths. Likewise also it is related

that in ancient times the tides of heat, swelling and overflowing from under Mt. Vesuvius, vomited forth fire from the mountain upon the neighboring country. Hence, what is called "sponge-stone" or "Pompeian pumice" appears to have been reduced by burning from another kind of stone to the condition of the kind which we see.

3. The kind of sponge-stone taken from this region is not produced everywhere else, but only about Aetna and among the hills of Mysia which the Greeks call the "Burnt District," and in other places of the same peculiar nature. Seeing that in such places there are found hot springs and warm vapor in excavations on the mountains, and that the ancients tell us that there were once fires spreading over the fields in those very regions, it seems to be certain that moisture has been extracted from the tufa and earth, by the force of fire, just as it is from limestone in kilns.

4. Therefore, when different and unlike things have been subjected to the action of fire and thus reduced to the same condition, if after this, while in a warm, dry state, they are suddenly saturated with water, there is an effervescence of the heat latent in the bodies of them all, and this makes them firmly unite and quickly assume the property of one solid mass.

There will still be the question why Tuscany, although it abounds in hot springs, does not furnish a powder out of which, on the same principle, a wall can be made which will set fast under water. I have therefore thought best to explain how this seems to be, before the question should be raised.

5. The same kinds of soil are not found in all places and countries alike, nor is stone found everywhere. Some soils are earthy; others gravelly, and again pebbly; in other places the material is sandy; in a word, the properties of the soil are as different and unlike as are the various countries. In particular, it may be observed that sandpits are hardly ever lacking in any place within the districts of Italy and Tuscany which are bounded by the Apennines; whereas across the Apennines toward the Adriatic none are found, and in Achaea and Asia Minor or, in short, across the sea, the very term is unknown. Hence it is not in all the places where boiling springs of hot water abound, that there is the same combination of favourable circumstances which has been described above. For things are produced in accordance with the will of nature; not to suit man's pleasure, but as it were by a chance distribution.

6. Therefore, where the mountains are not earthy but consist of soft stone, the force of the fire, passing through the fissures in the stone, sets it afire. The soft and delicate part is burned out, while the hard part is left. Consequently, while in Campania the burning of the earth makes ashes, in Tuscany the combustion of the stone makes carbuncular sand. Both are excellent in walls, but one is better to use for buildings on land, the other for piers under salt water. The Tuscan stone is softer in quality than tufa but harder than earth, and being thoroughly kindled by the violent heat from below, the result is the production in some places of the kind of sand called carbuncular.

Chapter 7
Stone

1. I have now spoken of lime and sand, with their varieties and points of excellence. Next comes the consideration of stone-quarries from which dimension stone and supplies of rubble to be used in building are taken and brought together. The stone in quarries is found to be of different and unlike qualities. In some it is soft: for example, in the environs of the city at the quarries of Grotta Rossa, Palla, Fidenae, and of the Alban hills; in others, it is medium, as at Tivoli, at Amiternum, or Mt. Soracte, and in quarries of this sort; in still others it is hard, as in lava quarries. There are also numerous other kinds: for instance, in Campania, red and black tufas; in Umbria, Picenum, and Venetia, white tufa which can be cut with a toothed saw, like wood.

2. All these soft kinds have the advantage that they can be easily worked as soon as they have

been taken from the quarries. Under cover they play their part well; but in open and exposed situations the frost and rime make them crumble, and they go to pieces. On the seacoast, too, the salt eats away and dissolves them, nor can they stand great heat either. But travertine and all stone of that class can stand injury whether from a heavy load laid upon it or from the weather; exposure to fire, however, it cannot bear, but splits and cracks to pieces at once. This is because in its natural composition there is but little moisture and not much of the earthy, but a great deal of air and of fire. Therefore, it is not only without the earthy and watery elements, but when fire, expelling the air from it by the operation and force of heat, penetrates into its inmost parts and occupies the empty spaces of the fissures, there comes a great glow and the stone is made to burn as fiercely as do the particles of fire itself.

3. There are also several quarries called Anician in the territory of Tarquinii, the stone being of the color of peperino. The principal workshops lie round the lake of Bolsena and in the prefecture of Statonia. This stone has innumerable good qualities. Neither the season of frost nor exposure to fire can harm it, but it remains solid and lasts to a great age, because there is only a little air and fire in its natural composition, a moderate amount of moisture, and a great deal of the earthy. Hence its structure is of close texture and solid, and so it cannot be injured by the weather or by the force of fire.

4. This may best be seen from monuments in the neighborhood of the town of Ferento which are made of stone from these quarries. Among them are large statues exceedingly well made, images of smaller size, and flowers and acanthus leaves gracefully carved. Old as these are, they look as fresh as if they were only just finished. Bronze workers, also, make molds for the casting of bronze out of stone from these quarries, and find it very useful in bronze-founding. If the quarries were only near Rome, all our buildings might well be constructed from the products of these workshops.

5. But since, on account of the proximity of the stone-quarries of Grotta Rossa, Palla, and the others that are nearest to the city, necessity drives us to make use of their products, we must proceed as follows, if we wish our work to be finished without flaws. Let the stone be taken from the quarry two years before building is to begin, and not in winter but in summer. Then let it lie exposed in an open place. Such stone as has been damaged by the two years of exposure should be used in the foundations. The rest, which remains unhurt, has passed the test of nature and will endure in those parts of the building which are above ground. This precaution should be observed, not only with dimension stone, but also with the rubble which is to be used in walls.

Chapter 9
Timber

[Timber will be hard to find close by Florence, but the principles noted here are useful. From point 5 below on, you can find qualities of different tree species.]

1. Timber should be felled between early autumn and the time when Favonius begins to blow. For in spring all trees become pregnant, and they are all employing their natural vigor in the production of leaves and of the fruits that return every year. The requirements of that season render them empty and swollen, and so they are weak and feeble because of their looseness of texture. This is also the case with women who have conceived. Their bodies are not considered perfectly healthy until the child is born; hence, pregnant slaves, when offered for sale, are not warranted sound, because the fetus as it grows within the body takes to itself as nourishment all the best qualities of the mother's food, and so the stronger it becomes as the full time for birth approaches, the less compact it allows that body to be from which it is produced. After the birth of the child, what was heretofore taken to promote the growth of another creature is now set free by the delivery of the newborn, and the channels being now empty and open, the body

will take it in by lapping up its juices, and thus becomes compact and returns to the natural strength which it had before.

2. On the same principle, with the ripening of the fruits in autumn the leaves begin to wither and the trees, taking up their sap from the earth through the roots, recover themselves and are restored to their former solid texture. But the strong air of winter compresses and solidifies them during the time above mentioned. Consequently, if the timber is felled on the principle and at the time above mentioned, it will be felled at the proper season.

3. In felling a tree we should cut into the trunk of it to the very heart, and then leave it standing so that the sap may drain out drop by drop throughout the whole of it. In this way the useless liquid which is within will run out through the sapwood instead of having to die in a mass of decay, thus spoiling the quality of the timber. Then and not till then, the tree being drained dry and the sap no longer dripping, let it be felled and it will be in the highest state of usefulness.

4. That this is so may be seen in the case of fruit trees. When these are tapped at the base and pruned, each at the proper time, they pour out from the heart through the tap holes all the superfluous and corrupting fluid which they contain, and thus the draining process makes them durable. But when the juices of trees have no means of escape, they clot and rot in them, making the trees hollow and good for nothing. Therefore, if the draining process does not exhaust them while they are still alive, there is no doubt that, if the same principle is followed in felling them for timber, they will last a long time and be very useful in buildings.

5. Trees vary and are unlike one another in their qualities. Thus it is with the oak, elm, poplar, cypress, fir, and the others which are most suitable to use in buildings. The oak, for instance, has not the efficacy of the fir, nor the cypress that of the elm. Nor in the case of other trees, is it natural that they should be alike; but the individual kinds are

effective in building, some in one way, some in another, owing to the different properties of their elements.

6. To begin with fir: it contains a great deal of air and fire with very little moisture and the earthy, so that, as its natural properties are of the lighter class, it is not heavy. Hence, its consistence being naturally stiff, it does not easily bend under the load, and keeps its straightness when used in the framework. But it contains so much heat that it generates and encourages decay, which spoils it; and it also kindles fire quickly because of the air in its body, which is so open that it takes in fire and so gives out a great flame.

7. The part which is nearest to the earth before the tree is cut down takes up moisture through the roots from the immediate neighborhood and hence is without knots and is "clear." But the upper part, on account of the great heat in it, throws up branches into the air through the knots; and this, when it is cut off about twenty feet from the ground and then hewn, is called "knotwood" because of its hardness and knottiness. The lowest part, after the tree is cut down and the sapwood of the same thrown away, is split up into four pieces and prepared for joiner's work, and so is called "clear-stock."

8. Oak, on the other hand, having enough and to spare of the earthy among its elements, and containing but little moisture, air, and fire, lasts for an unlimited period when buried in underground structures. It follows that when exposed to moisture, as its texture is not loose and porous, it cannot take in liquid on account of its compactness, but, withdrawing from the moisture, it resists it and warps, thus making cracks in the structures in which it is used.

9. The winter oak, being composed of a moderate amount of all the elements, is very useful in buildings, but when in a moist place, it takes in water to its center through its pores, its air and fire being expelled by the influence of the moisture, and so it rots. The Turkey oak and the beech, both containing a mixture of moisture, fire, and the

earthy, with a great deal of air, through this loose texture take in moisture to their center and soon decay. White and black poplar, as well as willow, linden, and the agnus castus, containing an abundance of fire and air, a moderate amount of moisture, and only a small amount of the earthy, are composed of a mixture which is proportionately rather light, and so they are of great service from their stiffness. Although on account of the mixture of the earthy in them they are not hard, yet their loose texture makes them gleaming white, and they are a convenient material to use in carving.

10. The alder, which is produced close by river banks, and which seems to be altogether useless as building material, has really excellent qualities. It is composed of a very large proportion of air and fire, not much of the earthy, and only a little moisture. Hence, in swampy places, alder piles driven close together beneath the foundations of buildings take in the water which their own consistence lacks and remain imperishable forever, supporting structures of enormous weight and keeping them from decay. Thus a material which cannot last even a little while above ground, endures for a long time when covered with moisture.

11. One can see this at its best in Ravenna; for there all the buildings, both public and private, have piles of this sort beneath their foundations. The elm and the ash contain a very great amount of moisture, a minimum of air and fire, and a moderate mixture of the earthy in their composition. When put in shape for use in buildings they are tough and, having no stiffness on account of the weight of moisture in them, soon bend. But when they become dry with age, or are allowed to lose their sap and die standing in the open, they get harder, and from their toughness supply a strong material for dowels to be used in joints and other articulations.

12. The hornbeam, which has a very small amount of fire and of the earthy in its composition, but a very great proportion of air and moisture, is not a wood that breaks easily, and is very convenient to handle. Hence, the Greeks call it "zygia," because they make of it yokes for their draught-animals, and their word for yoke is ξυγά. Cypress and pine are also just as admirable; for although they contain an abundance of moisture mixed with an equivalent composed of all the other elements, and so are apt to warp when used in buildings on account of this superfluity of moisture, yet they can be kept to a great age without rotting, because the liquid contained within their substances has a bitter taste which by its pungency prevents the entrance of decay or of those little creatures which are destructive. Hence, buildings made of these kinds of wood last for an unending period of time.

13. The cedar and the juniper tree have the same uses and good qualities, but, while the cypress and pine yield resin, from the cedar is produced an oil called cedar-oil. Books as well as other things smeared with this are not hurt by worms or decay. The foliage of this tree is like that of the cypress but the grain of the wood is straight. The statue of Diana in the temple at Ephesus is made of it, and so are the coffered ceilings both there and in all other famous fanes, because that wood is everlasting. The tree grows chiefly in Crete, Africa, and in some districts of Syria.

14. The larch, known only to the people of the towns on the banks of the river Po and the shores of the Adriatic, is not only preserved from decay and the worm by the great bitterness of its sap, but also it cannot be kindled with fire nor ignite of itself, unless like stone in a limekiln it is burned with other wood. And even then it does not take fire nor produce burning coals, but after a long time it slowly consumes away. This is because there is a very small proportion of the elements of fire and air in its composition, which is a dense and solid mass of moisture and the earthy, so that it has no open pores through which fire can find its way; but it repels the force of fire and does not let itself be harmed by it quickly. Further, its weight will not let it float in water, so that when transported it is loaded on shipboard or on rafts made of fir.

15. It is worth while to know how this wood was discovered. The divine Caesar, being with his army in the neighborhood of the Alps, and having ordered the towns to furnish supplies, the inhabitants of a fortified stronghold there, called Larignum, trusting in the natural strength of their defenses, refused to obey his command. So the general ordered his forces to the assault. In front of the gate of this stronghold there was a tower, made of beams of this wood laid in alternating directions at right angles to each other, like a funeral pyre, and built high, so that they could drive off an attacking party by throwing stakes and stones from the top. When it was observed that they had no other missiles than stakes, and that these could not be hurled very far from the wall on account of the weight, orders were given to approach and to throw bundles of brushwood and lighted torches at this outwork. These the soldiers soon got together.

16. The flames soon kindled the brushwood which lay about that wooden structure and, rising towards heaven, made everybody think that the whole pile had fallen. But when the fire had burned itself out and subsided, and the tower appeared to view entirely uninjured, Caesar in amazement gave orders that they should be surrounded with a palisade, built beyond the range of missiles. So the townspeople were frightened into surrendering, and were then asked where that wood came from which was not harmed by fire. They pointed to trees of the kind under discussion, of which there are very great numbers in that vicinity. And so, as that stronghold was called Larignum, the wood was called larch. It is transported by way of the Po to Ravenna, and is to be had in Fano, Pesaro, Ancona, and the other towns in that neighborhood. If there were only a ready method of carrying this material to Rome, it would be of the greatest use in buildings; if not for general purposes, yet at least if the boards used in the eaves running round blocks of houses were made of it, the buildings would be free from the danger of fire spreading across to them, because such boards can neither take fire from flames or from burning coals, nor ignite spontaneously.

17. The leaves of these trees are like those of the pine; timber from them comes in long lengths, is as easily wrought in joiner's work as is the clear-wood of fir, and contains a liquid resin, of the color of Attic honey, which is good for consumptives.

With regard to the different kinds of timber, I have now explained of what natural properties they appear to be composed, and how they were produced. It remains to consider the question why the highland fir, as it is called in Rome, is inferior, while the lowland fir is extremely useful in buildings so far as durability is concerned; and further to explain how it is that their bad or good qualities seem to be due to the peculiarities of their neighborhood, so that this subject may be clearer to those who examine it.

Book 10

[This book starts with some ideas about fiscal responsibility, a topic that has timeless importance.]

Introduction

1. In the famous and important Greek city of Ephesus there is said to be an ancient ancestral law, the terms of which are severe, but its justice is not inequitable. When an architect accepts the charge of a public work, he has to promise what the cost of it will be. His estimate is handed to the magistrate, and his property is pledged as security until the work is done. When it is finished, if the outlay agrees with his statement, he is complimented by decrees and marks of honor. If no more than a fourth has to be added to his estimate, it is furnished by the treasury and no penalty is inflicted. But when more than one fourth has to be spent in addition on the work, the money required to finish it is taken from his property.

2. Would to God that this were also a law of the Roman people, not merely for public, but also for private buildings. For the ignorant would no longer run riot with impunity, but men who are well

qualified by an exact scientific training would unquestionably adopt the profession of architecture. Gentlemen would not be misled into limitless and prodigal expenditure, even to ejectments from their estates, and the architects themselves could be forced, by fear of the penalty, to be more careful in calculating and stating the limit of expense, so that gentlemen would procure their buildings for that which they had expected, or by adding only a little more. It is true that men who can afford to devote four hundred thousand to a work may hold on, if they have to add another hundred thousand, from the pleasure which the hope of finishing it gives them; but if they are loaded with a fifty per cent increase, or with an even greater expense, they lose hope, sacrifice what they have already spent, and are compelled to leave off, broken in fortune and in spirit.

3. This fault appears not only in the matter of buildings, but also in the shows given by magistrates, whether of gladiators in the forum or of plays on the stage. Here neither delay nor postponement is permissible, but the necessities of the case require that everything should be ready at a fixed time,—the seats for the audience, the awning drawn over them, and whatever, in accordance with the customs of the stage, is provided by machinery to please the eye of the people. These matters require careful thought and planning by a well-trained intellect; for none of them can be accomplished without machinery, and without hard study skillfully applied in various ways.

4. Therefore, since such are our traditions and established practices, it is obviously fitting that the plans should be worked out carefully, and with the greatest attention, before the structures are begun. Consequently, as we have no law or customary practice to compel this, and as every year both praetors and aediles have to provide machinery for the festivals, I have thought it not out of place, Emperor, since I have treated of buildings in the earlier books, to set forth and teach in this, which forms the final conclusion of my treatise, the principles which govern machines.

Chapter 1

[As part of the challenge in the game is to consider mechanisms for moving and hoisting materials, this section will be of interest. Referring to Cotterell and Kamminga's *Mechanics of Pre-Industrial Technology* may help you visualize these tools.]

Machines and Implements

1. A machine is a combination of timbers fastened together, chiefly efficacious in moving great weights. Such a machine is set in motion on scientific principles in circular rounds, which the Greeks call κυλικη κίνησις. There is, however, a class intended for climbing, termed in Greek ἀκροβατικόν, another worked by air, which with them is called πνευματικόν, and a third for hoisting; this the Greeks named βαρουλκός. In the climbing class are machines so disposed that one can safely climb up high, by means of timbers set up on end and connected by crossbeams, in order to view operations. In the pneumatic class, air is forced by pressure to produce sounds and tones as in an ὄργανον [organ].

2. In the hoisting class, heavy weights are removed by machines which raise them up and set them in position. The climbing machine displays no scientific principle, but merely a spirit of daring. It is held together by dowels and crossbeams and twisted lashings and supporting props. A machine that gets its motive power by pneumatic pressure will produce pretty effects by scientific refinements. But the hoisting machine has opportunities for usefulness which are greater and full of grandeur, and it is of the highest efficacy when used with intelligence.

[Here the engines are machines that use interlocking gears—anisocycli, the scorpio, was a type of military tool used in sieges.]

3. Some of these act on the principle of the μηχανή [machine], others on that of the ὄργανον. The difference between "machines" and "engines" is obviously this, that machines need more workmen and greater power to make them take effect, as for instance ballistae and the beams of presses.

Engines, on the other hand, accomplish their purpose at the intelligent touch of a single workman, as the scorpio or anisocycli when they are turned. Therefore engines, as well as machines, are, in principle, practical necessities, without which nothing can be unattended with difficulties.

4. All machinery is derived from nature, and is founded on the teaching and instruction of the revolution of the firmament. Let us but consider the connected revolutions of the sun, the moon, and the five planets, without the revolution of which, due to mechanism, we should not have had the alternation of day and night, nor the ripening of fruits. Thus, when our ancestors had seen that this was so, they took their models from nature, and by imitating them were led on by divine facts, until they perfected the contrivances which are so serviceable in our life. Some things, with a view to greater convenience, they worked out by means of machines and their revolutions, others by means of engines, and so, whatever they found to be useful for investigations, for the arts, and for established practices, they took care to improve step by step on scientific principles.

[Here we are being reminded of basic tools that became parts of wine and oil presses and weaving looms, as well as the use of wind, water, and animals for power, axles for carts, and so on.]

5. Let us take first a necessary invention, such as clothing, and see how the combination of warp and woof on the loom, which does its work on the principle of an engine, not only protects the body by covering it, but also gives it honorable apparel. We should not have had food in abundance unless yokes and ploughs for oxen, and for all draught animals, had been invented. If there had been no provision of windlasses, press beams, and levers for presses, we could not have had the shining oil, nor the fruit of the vine to give us pleasure, and these things could not have been transported on land without the invention of the mechanism of carts or wagons, nor on the sea without that of ships.

6. The discovery of the method of testing weights by steelyards and balances saves us from fraud, by introducing honest practices into life. There are also innumerable ways of employing machinery about which it seems unnecessary to speak, since they are at hand every day; such as mills, blacksmiths' bellows, carriages, gigs, turning lathes, and other things which are habitually used as general conveniences. Hence, we shall begin by explaining those that rarely come to hand, so that they may be understood.

Chapter 2
Hoisting Machines
[The hoist described below is also described in your text, and illustrations can be found online. It is essentially a tripod of wood and cord made steady so a pulley can be suspended and used to lift weights by turning a hand-cranked axle.]

1. First we shall treat of those machines which are of necessity made ready when temples and public buildings are to be constructed. Two timbers are provided, strong enough for the weight of the load. They are fastened together at the upper end by a bolt, then spread apart at the bottom, and so set up, being kept upright by ropes attached at the upper ends and fixed at intervals all round. At the top is fastened a block, which some call a "rechamus." In the block two sheaves are enclosed, turning on axles. The traction rope is carried over the sheave at the top, then let fall and passed round a sheave in a block below. Then it is brought back to a sheave at the bottom of the upper block, and so it goes down to the lower block, where it is fastened through a hole in that block. The other end of the rope is brought back and down between the legs of the machine.

[The windlass is an X-shaped handle like the one you might use to take off nuts when changing a car tire. The shape has leverage and makes it easier to turn heavier weights.]

2. Socket-pieces are nailed to the hinder faces of the squared timbers at the point where they are spread apart, and the ends of the windlass are inserted into them so that the axles may turn freely. Close to each end of the windlass are two

holes, so adjusted that handspikes can be fitted into them. To the bottom of the lower block are fastened shears made of iron, whose prongs are brought to bear upon the stones, which have holes bored in them. When one end of the rope is fastened to the windlass, and the latter is turned round by working the handspikes, the rope winds round the windlass, gets taut, and thus it raises the load to the proper height and to its place in the work.

[The trispast uses three pulleys and the pentaspast has five ropes.]

3. This kind of machinery, revolving with three sheaves, is called a trispast. When there are two sheaves turning in the block beneath and three in the upper, the machine is termed a pentaspast. But if we have to furnish machines for heavier loads, we must use timbers of greater length and thickness, providing them with correspondingly large bolts at the top, and windlasses turning at the bottom. When these are ready, let forestays be attached and left lying slack in front; let the backstays be carried over the shoulders of the machine to some distance, and, if there is nothing to which they can be fastened, sloping piles should be driven, the ground rammed down all round to fix them firmly, and the ropes made fast to them.

[Here you have a description of how to anchor cords in place as well as ways to turn an axle to help lift a heavy load.]

4. A block should then be attached by a stout cord to the top of the machine, and from that point a rope should be carried to a pile, and to a block tied to the pile. Let the rope be put in round the sheave of this block, and brought back to the block that is fastened at the top of the machine. Round its sheave the rope should be passed, and then should go down from the top, and back to the windlass, which is at the bottom of the machine, and there be fastened. The windlass is now to be turned by means of the handspikes, and it will raise the machine of itself without danger. Thus, a machine of the larger kind will be set in position, with its ropes in their places about it, and its stays attached

to the piles. Its blocks and traction ropes are arranged as described above.

5. But if the loads of material for the work are still more colossal in size and weight, we shall not entrust them to a windlass, but set in an axle-tree, held by sockets as the windlass was, and carrying on its centre a large drum, which some term a wheel, but the Greeks call it ἀμφίεσις or περιθήκιον.

6. And the blocks in such machines are not arranged in the same, but in a different manner; for the rows of sheaves in them are doubled, both at the bottom and at the top. The traction rope is passed through a hole in the lower block, in such a way that the two ends of the rope are of equal length when it is stretched out, and both portions are held there at the lower block by a cord which is passed round them and lashed so that they cannot come out either to the right or the left. Then the ends of the rope are brought up into the block at the top from the outside, and passed down over its lower sheaves, and so return to the bottom, and are passed from the inside to the sheaves in the lowest block, and then are brought up on the right and left, and return to the top and round the highest set of sheaves.

7. Passing over these from the outside, they are then carried to the right and left of the drum on the axle-tree, and are tied there so as to stay fast. Then another rope is wound round the drum and carried to a capstan, and when that is turned, it turns the drum and the axle-tree, the ropes get taut as they wind round regularly, and thus they raise the loads smoothly and with no danger. But if a larger drum is placed either in the middle or at one side, without any capstan, men can tread in it and accomplish the work more expeditiously.

8. There is also another kind of machine, ingenious enough and easy to use with speed, but only experts can work with it. It consists of a single timber, which is set up and held in place by stays on four sides. Two cheeks are nailed on below the stays, a block is fastened by ropes above the cheeks, and a straight piece of wood about two feet long, six digits wide, and four digits thick, is put under

the block. The blocks used have each three rows of sheaves side by side. Hence three traction ropes are fastened at the top of the machine. Then they are brought to the block at the bottom, and passed from the inside round the sheaves that are nearest the top of it. Then they are brought back to the upper block, and passed inwards from outside round the sheaves nearest the bottom.

9. On coming down to the block at the bottom, they are carried round its second row of sheaves from the inside to the outside, and brought back to the second row at the top, passing round it and returning to the bottom; then from the bottom they are carried to the summit, where they pass round the highest row of sheaves, and then return to the bottom of the machine. At the foot of the machine a third block is attached. The Greeks call it ἐπάγων, but our people "artemon." This block fastened at the foot of the machine has three sheaves in it, round which the ropes are passed and then delivered to men to pull. Thus, three rows of men, pulling without a capstan, can quickly raise the load to the top.

10. This kind of machine is called a polyspast, because of the many revolving sheaves to which its dexterity and despatch are due. There is also this advantage in the erection of only a single timber, that by previously inclining it to the right or left as much as one wishes, the load can be set down at one side.

All these kinds of machinery described above are, in their principles, suited not only to the purposes mentioned, but also to the loading and unloading of ships, some kinds being set upright, and others placed horizontally on revolving platforms. On the same principle, ships can be hauled ashore by means of arrangements of ropes and blocks used on the ground, without setting up timbers.

11. It may also not be out of place to explain the ingenious procedure of Chersiphron. Desiring to convey the shafts for the temple of Diana at Ephesus from the stone quarries, and not trusting to carts, lest their wheels should be engulfed on

account of the great weights of the load and the softness of the roads in the plain, he tried the following plan. Using four-inch timbers, he joined two of them, each as long as the shaft, with two crosspieces set between them, dovetailing all together, and then leaded iron gudgeons shaped like dovetails into the ends of the shafts, as dowels are leaded, and in the woodwork he fixed rings to contain the pivots, and fastened wooden cheeks to the ends. The pivots, being enclosed in the rings, turned freely. So, when yokes of oxen began to draw the four-inch frame, they made the shaft revolve constantly, turning it by means of the pivots and rings.

12. When they had thus transported all the shafts, and it became necessary to transport the architraves, Chersiphron's son Metagenes extended the same principle from the transportation of the shafts to the bringing down of the architraves. He made wheels, each about twelve feet in diameter, and enclosed the ends of the architraves in the wheels. In the ends he fixed pivots and rings in the same way. So when the four-inch frames were drawn by oxen, the wheels turned on the pivots enclosed in the rings, and the architraves, which were enclosed like axles in the wheels, soon reached the building, in the same way as the shafts. The rollers used for smoothing the walks in palaestrae will serve as an example of this method. But it could not have been employed unless the distance had been short; for it is not more than eight miles from the stone-quarries to the temple, and there is no hill, but an uninterrupted plain.

13. In our own times, however, when the pedestal of the colossal Apollo in his temple had cracked with age, they were afraid that the statue would fall and be broken, and so they contracted for the cutting of a pedestal from the same quarries. The contract was taken by one Paconius. This pedestal was twelve feet long, eight feet wide, and six feet high. Paconius, with confident pride, did not transport it by the method of Metagenes, but determined to make a machine of a different sort, though on the same principle.

14. He made wheels of about fifteen feet in diameter, and in these wheels he enclosed the ends of the stone; then he fastened two-inch crossbars from wheel to wheel round the stone, encompassing it, so that there was an interval of not more than one foot between bar and bar. Then he coiled a rope round the bars, yoked up his oxen, and began to draw on the rope. Consequently as it uncoiled, it did indeed cause the wheels to turn, but it could not draw them in a line straight along the road, but kept swerving out to one side. Hence it was necessary to draw the machine back again. Thus, by this drawing to and fro, Paconius got into such financial embarrassment that he became insolvent.

15. I will digress a bit and explain how these stone-quarries were discovered. Pixodorus was a shepherd who lived in that vicinity. When the people of Ephesus were planning to build the temple of Diana in marble, and debating whether to get the marble from Paros, Proconnesus, Heraclea, or Thasos, Pixodorus drove out his sheep and was feeding his flock in that very spot. Then two rams ran at each other, and, each passing the other, one of them, after his charge, struck his horns against a rock, from which a fragment of extremely white color was dislodged. So it is said that Pixodorus left his sheep in the mountains and ran down to Ephesus carrying the fragment, since that very thing was the question of the moment. Therefore they immediately decreed honors to him and changed his name, so that instead of Pixodorus he should be called Evangelus. And to this day the chief magistrate goes out to that very spot every month and offers sacrifice to him, and if he does not, he is punished.

Chapter 3
The Elements of Motion

1. I have briefly set forth what I thought necessary about the principles of hoisting machines. In them two different things, unlike each other, work together, as elements of their motion and power, to produce these effects. One of them is the right line, which the Greeks term εὐθεια; the other is the circle, which the Greeks call κυκλωτή; but in point of fact, neither rectilinear without circular motion, nor revolutions, without rectilinear motion, can accomplish the raising of loads. I will explain this, so that it may be understood.

2. As centers, axles are inserted into the sheaves, and these are fastened in the blocks; a rope carried over the sheaves, drawn straight down, and fastened to a windlass, causes the load to move upward from its place as the handspikes are turned. The pivots of this windlass, lying as centers in right lines in its socket-pieces, and the handspikes inserted in its holes, make the load rise when the ends of the windlass revolve in a circle like a lathe. Just so, when an iron lever is applied to a weight which a great many hands cannot move, with the fulcrum, which the Greeks call ὑπομόχλιον, lying as a center in a right line under the lever, and with the tongue of the lever placed under the weight, one man's strength, bearing down upon the head of it, heaves up the weight.

3. For, as the shorter fore part of the lever goes under the weight from the fulcrum that forms the center, the head of it, which is farther away from that center, on being depressed, is made to describe a circular movement, and thus by pressure brings to an equilibrium the weight of a very great load by means of a few hands. Again, if the tongue of an iron lever is placed under a weight, and its head is not pushed down, but, on the contrary, is heaved up, the tongue, supported on the surface of the ground, will treat that as the weight, and the edge of the weight itself as the fulcrum. Thus, not so easily as by pushing down, but by motion in the opposite direction, the weight of the load will nevertheless be raised. If, therefore, the tongue of a lever lying on a fulcrum goes too far under the weight, and its head exerts its pressure too near the center, it will not be able to elevate the weight, nor can it do so unless, as described above, the length of the lever is brought to equilibrium by the depression of its head.

4. This may be seen from the balances that we call steelyards. When the handle is set as a center

close to the end from which the scale hangs, and the counterpoise is moved along towards the other arm of the beam, shifting from point to point as it goes farther or even reaches the extremity, a small and inferior weight becomes equal to a very heavy object that is being weighed, on account of the equilibrium that is due to the levelling of the beam. Thus, as it withdraws from the center, a small and comparatively light counterpoise, slowly turning the scale, makes a greater amount of weight rise gently upwards from below.

5. So, too, the pilot of the biggest merchantman, grasping the steering oar by its handle, which the Greeks call οἴαξ, and with one hand bringing it to the turning point, according to the rules of his art, by pressure about a center, can turn the ship, although she may be laden with a very large or even enormous burden of merchandise and provisions. And when her sails are set only halfway up the mast, a ship cannot run quickly; but when the yard is hoisted to the top, she makes much quicker progress, because then the sails get the wind, not when they are too close to the heel of the mast, which represents the center, but when they have moved farther away from it to the top.

6. As a lever thrust under a weight is harder to manage, and does not put forth its strength, if the pressure is exerted at the center, but easily raises the weight when the extreme end of it is pushed down, so sails that are only halfway up have less effect, but when they get farther away from the center, and are hoisted to the very top of the mast, the pressure at the top forces the ship to make greater progress, though the wind is no stronger but just the same. Again, take the case of oars, which are fastened to the holes by loops,—when they are pushed forward and drawn back by the hand, if the ends of the blades are at some distance from the center, the oars foam with the waves of the sea and drive the ship forward in a straight line with a mighty impulse, while her prow cuts through the rare water.

7. And when the heaviest burdens are carried on poles by four or six porters at a time, they find the centers of balance at the very middle of the poles, so that, by distributing the dead weight of the burden according to a definitely proportioned division, each laborer may have an equal share to carry on his neck. For the poles, from which the straps for the burden of the four porters hang, are marked off at their centers by nails, to prevent the straps from slipping to one side. If they shift beyond the mark at the center, they weigh heavily upon the place to which they have come nearer, like the weight of a steelyard when it moves from the point of equilibrium towards the end of the weighing apparatus.

8. In the same way, oxen have an equal draught when their yoke is adjusted at its middle by the yoke strap to the pole. But when their strength is not the same, and the stronger outdoes the other, the strap is shifted so as to make one side of the yoke longer, which helps the weaker ox. Thus, in the case of both poles and yokes, when the straps are not fastened at the middle, but at one side, the farther the strap moves from the middle, the shorter it makes one side, and the longer the other. So, if both ends are carried round in circles, using as a center the point to which the strap has been brought, the longer end will describe a larger, and the shorter end a smaller circle.

9. Just as smaller wheels move harder and with greater difficulty than larger ones, so, in the case of the poles and yokes, the parts where the interval from center to end is less, bear down hard upon the neck, but where the distance from the same center is greater, they ease the burden both for draught and carriage. As in all these cases motion is obtained by means of right lines at the centre and by circles, so also farm waggons, travelling carriages, drums, mills, screws, scorpiones, ballistae, pressbeams, and all other machines, produce the results intended, on the same principles, by turning about a rectilinear axis and by the revolution of a circle.

To look at the entire original text, see the Project Gutenberg website or the Perseus website at Tufts.

Appendix

Aesthetics: The study and perceptions of beauty and the theories that arise from it, including emotional and psychological responses to beauty.

Arti or *Corporazioni:* In the sense of Arte della Seta, it is a type of guild. A craft and political-social organization. These wielded great social influence and power in Florence at this time.

Capomaestro: Foreman of a construction project.

Compass: A draftsman's compass is shaped like an upside-down V, with one arm that can expand. One arm is fixed to the surface while the other lightly touches the surface of plaster, paper, or wall and can scratch into it or draw on it an arc or a circle while rotating around the fixed arm.

Compressive strength: The amount of weight a material can bear before fracturing.

Curia: The senate in ancient Rome; a term for the papal court and/or administration.

Drum: Dome, or also cathedral.

Duomo: A round or multisided foundation from which a dome springs (rises).

Festa: Feast, holiday, party.

Firenze: Florence.

Gnomon: Standard (a banner or flag with crest).

Gonfalone: The upright bar or pin on a sundial that creates the shadow.

Gonfaloniere: Civic magistrate or leader.

Legnaiolo: Carpenter or wood worker.

Opera del Duomo: The term means any activity, action, or work that is directed for a particular purpose. It can also mean the result of someone's action, or the body of works that someone creates. In this game, the term is often shortened just to "Opera" (and you will find it even today with regard to this cathedral as the Opera del Santa Maria del Fiore, since it was the members of the Opera who organized, financed, and directed the construction of the church and who now run the museum.

Palazzo: Palace or large building.

Palio: Long fabric, often on a pole, that is highly decorated and given as a prize to the winners of races or competitions. It also means to put something in competition, and is the name given to the horse races run in some Italian towns around a piazza (no saddles, and no course lanes) for which that decorated fabric is the prize.

Papal nunzio: Secretary, legal and otherwise, to the pope.

Plumb bob: A weight (sometimes teardrop shaped) suspended from a cord to help test if a wall or another object is properly vertical.

Priori: At this time in Florence a magistrate, but also a term for a superior in a monastery.

FIGURE 11 Pantheon, Rome, internal view.

Quartieri:	Neighborhood.
Santa Maria del Fiore:	St Mary of the Flowers.
Signoria:	Seat of Florence's government.
Spandrel:	The triangular space between the top of an arch and the frame or support above it.
T-square:	A ruler with a perpendicular piece at the top that can be put over the side of a drawing board so that the ruler can be moved up and down while staying horizontal.
Tensile strength:	The amount of force needed to pull a rope, wire, or a structural beam to the breaking point. (Check out the ScienceDaily website and search for articles on tensile strength.)
Vault:	An arched roof or ceiling, or the arch stretching from one column to another.

FIGURE 12 Pantheon, Rome, external details.

FIGURE 13 Pantheon, Rome, internal details.

IMAGES OF ROMAN WORKS PEOPLE WOULD HAVE KNOWN

In addition to figures 11–13, you can find others in a separate document provided by your professor.

Figure 11 shows both the coffered ceiling (receding boxes—thus lightening the interior surface because, since not solid throughout, it weighs less) and the oculus.

Figure 12 and figure 13 show good examples of how bricks were used in multiple directions and to make supporting arches and vaults.

ADDITIONAL IMAGES THAT YOU MIGHT WANT TO SEARCH FOR:

Colosseum, Rome, Italy
Pont du Gard, Nimes, France
Hagia Sophia, Istanbul, Turkey

Dome of the Rock, Jerusalem, Israel
Baptistry of San Giovanni, Pisa, Italy
St Front, Perigueux, France

Supplemental Documents

RESOURCES ON THE WEB
Alighieri, Dante, *The Divine Comedy*
This can be found on the Gutenberg website, or pick up a copy in your library.

This may be useful for scholars looking to see connections between the construction plans (and the model) with the organization of the first book of this work, the *Inferno*, or perhaps to mine these works looking at how Dante describes people, behaviors, and professions.

The works of Archimedes and Euclid provide examples of calculations and illustrations of machines and tools that people would have known about and used.

Archimedes
There are several examples of Archimedes's machines to be found on the internet, but you might also find them via the following books:

Peter James and Nick Thorpe, *Ancient Inventions* (New York: Ballantine Books, 1994).
J. G. Landels, *Engineering in the Ancient World* (Berkeley: University of California Press, 1978).

Euclid, *Elements*
A quick internet search will provide various editions of Euclid's *Elements*, or it can be found in your library.

Lucretius, *On the Nature of Things*
This can be found at the MIT classics website or in your college library.

This work was newly discovered at this time, and its ideas shook up conventional thinking.

Opera di Santa Maria del Fiore Florence—Years of the Cupola 1417–1436.
Documents. Edited by Haines.

This website is full of documents related to the construction of the dome including types of workers, materials ordered and delivered (or not), and in some cases costs of labor and materials.

SOURCES
Each of the sources listed below provides background historical information either on the period or on the project of the dome, or is a primary document from which some of our texts were excerpted. They can help you deepen your knowledge of the period or the project, or provide illustrations or additional information about building techniques.

Alberti, Leon Battista. *On the Art of Building in Ten Books*. Translated by Joseph Rykwert, Neil Leach, and Robert Tavernor. Cambridge, Mass.: MIT Press, 1988.
Battisti, Eugenio, and Filippo Brunelleschi. *Filippo Brunelleschi: The Complete Work*. New York: Rizzoli, 1981.
Belting, Hans, and Deborah Lucas Schneider. *Florence and Baghdad: Renaissance Art and Arab Science*. Cambridge, Mass.: Belknap Press of Harvard University Press, 2011.
Bergstein, Mary. *The Sculpture of Nanni di Banco*. Princeton, N.J.: Princeton University Press, 2000.
Brucker, Gene. *The Civic World of Early Renaissance Florence*. Princeton, N.J.: Princeton University Press, 1977. (This can also be found online.)
Bruni, Leonardo. "Panegyric of Florence" (ca. 1404). In *Images of Quattrocento Florence: Selected Writings in Literature, History, and Art*, edited by Stefano Ugo Baldassarri and Arielle Saiber, 39–43. New Haven, Conn.: Yale University Press, 2000.

Corazzi, Roberto, and Giuseppe Conti. *Il Segreto della Cupola del Brunelleschi a Firenze/The Secret of Brunelleschi's Dome in Florence*. Florence: Angelo Pontecorboli Editore, 2011.

Cotterell, Brian, and Johan Kamminga. *Mechanics of Pre-industrial Technology: An Introduction to the Mechanics of Ancient and Traditional Material Culture*. Cambridge: Cambridge University Press, 1992.

Cowan, H. J. "A History of Masonry and Concrete Domes in Building Construction." *Building and Environment* 12 (1977): 1–24.

Dati, Goro. "The Structure of the Florentine Government." In *Images of Quattrocento Florence: Selected Writings in Literature, History, and Art*, edited by Stefano Ugo Baldassarri and Arielle Saiber, 44–54. New Haven, Conn.: Yale University Press, 2000.

Edgerton, Samuel Y., Jr. *The Renaissance Rediscovery of Linear Perspective*. New York: Basic Books, 1975. (This can also be found online.)

Fanelli, Giovanni, and Michele Fanelli. *Brunelleschi's Cupola: Past and Present of an Architectural Masterpiece*. Florence: Mandragora, 2004.

Galloway, James. "Perspectives on Mathematics in Art History." *Math Horizons* 16, no. 2 (November 2008): 16–19 (a good source for information on perspective).

Galluzzi, Paolo. *Mechanical Marvels: Invention in the Age of Leonardo* [New York, World Financial Center, Liberty Street Gallery, October 24, 1997–March 1, 1998]. Florence: Giunti, 1997.

Goldthwaite, Richard. *The Building of Renaissance Florence: An Economic and Social History*. Baltimore: Johns Hopkins University Press, 1980.

Granger, Frank, ed. *Vitruvius: On Architecture*. 2 vols. Cambridge, Mass.: Harvard University Press, 1962.

Haines, Margaret. "Brunelleschi and Bureaucracy: The Tradition of Public Patronage at the Florentine Cathedral." *I Tatti Studies in the Italian Renaissance* 3 (1989): 89–125.

———. "Myth and Management in the Construction of Brunelleschi's Cupola." *I Tatti Studies in the Italian Renaissance* 14/15 (2011–12): 47–101.

Hyman, Isabelle, ed. *Brunelleschi in Perspective*. Englewood Cliffs, N.J.: Prentice-Hall, 1974.

Ingold, Tim, *Making: Anthropology, Archaeology, Art and Architecture*. London: Routledge, 2013.

Jones, Barry, Andrea Sereni, and Massimo Ricci. "Building Brunelleschi's Dome: A Practical Methodology Verified by Experiment." *Journal of the Society of Architectural Historians* 69, no. 1 (2010): 39–61.

King, Ross. *Brunelleschi's Dome: How a Renaissance Genius Reinvented Architecture*. New York: Walker, 2000.

Kozak-Holland, Mark, and C. Procter. "Florence Duomo Project (1420–1436): Learning Best Project Management Practice from History." *International Journal of Project Management* 32 (2014): 242–55.

Mainstone, Rowland. "Brunelleschi's Dome." *Architectural Review*, September 1977, 157–66.

Musa, Mark. *The Portable Dante*. New York: Penguin Books, 2003.

Najemy, John. *A History of Florence 1200–1575*. Malden, Mass.: Blackwell, 2006.

Prager, Frank D., and Gustina Scaglia. *Brunelleschi: Studies of His Technology and Inventions*. Cambridge, Mass.: MIT Press, 1970.

Saalman, Howard. *Filippo Brunelleschi: The Cupola of Santa Maria del Fiore*. London: A. Zwemmer, 1980.

Salutati, Coluccio. "A Defense of the Roman Origins of Florence." In *Images of Quattrocento Florence: Selected Writings in Literature, History, and Art*, edited by Stefano Ugo Baldassarri and Arielle Saiber, 3–11. New Haven, Conn.: Yale University Press, 2000.

Schneider, Deborah Lucas. *Florence and Baghdad: Renaissance Art and Arab Science*. Cambridge, Mass.: Belknap Press of Harvard University Press, 2011.

Smith, Christine. *Architecture in the Culture of Early Humanism: Ethics, Aesthetics, and*

Eloquence, 1400–1470. New York: Oxford University Press, 1991.

Staley, John Edgcumbe. *The Guilds of Florence, by Edgcumbe Staley: llustrated after Miniatures in Illuminated Manuscripts and Florentine Woodcuts, with Bibliographical and Chronological Tables*. London: Methuen, 1906.

Tacconi, Marica. *Cathedral and Civic Ritual in Late Medieval and Renaissance Florence: The Service Books of Santa Maria del Fiore*. Cambridge: Cambridge University Press, 2005.

Trexler, Richard. *Public Life in Renaissance Florence*. Ithaca, N.Y.: Cornell University Press, 1991.

Walker, Paul Robert. *The Feud That Sparked the Renaissance: How Brunelleschi and Ghiberti Changed the Art World*. New York: HarperCollins, 2004.

Westfall, Carroll William. *Architecture, Liberty and Civic Order: Architectural Theories from Vitruvius to Jefferson and Beyond*. London: Routledge, 2015.

White, John. *Art and Architecture in Italy: 1250–1400*. Edited by Nikolaus Pevsner. Baltimore, Md.: Penguin Books, 1966.

Wood-Brown, J. C. *The Builders of Florence*. New York: E. P. Dutton, 1907.

Acknowledgments

This project has had a long gestation, and many people have shared their time and wisdom to help the project come to fruition. I am grateful to all my reacting colleagues who participated in the workshop session at the first Game Development Conference (GDC) at Central Michigan University in July 2012 and who asked the hard questions that gave the game structure and focus; and to those who play-tested the game at the GDC at Simpson in 2014, and at the Barnard Summer Institute in 2018. The ideas and feedback offered has been invaluable. Special thanks go to Dorothea Herreiner for invaluable references and hospitality in Florence and to Martina Saltamacchia, Paul Wright, and Lisa Bauman for additional references and suggestions. Thanks are also due to Marie Gasper-Hulvat and Mary Beth Looney and their students for playtesting this game and providing critical feedback. Throughout the development process, several reviewers, including Jace Weaver and Matt Wranovix, have provided invaluable suggestions and critique; and this book would not have reached the finish line without guidance and assistance from the folks at the University of North Carolina Press and Westchester Publishing Services. Thank you all. Finally, I am grateful to David Eick for his encouragement in pursing this project.

CPSIA information can be obtained
at www.ICGtesting.com
Printed in the USA
LVHW061718151119
637496LV00008B/169/P

9 781469 653396